pasta sauces

simple recipes for delicious food every day

r**p**s

RYLAND PETERS & SMALL
LONDON • NEW YORK

Senior Designer Toni Kay
Production Meskerem Berhane
Art Director Leslie Harrington
Editorial Director Julia Charles

Indexer Hilary Bird

First published in 2014
by Ryland Peters & Small
20–21 Jockey's Fields
London WC1R 4BW
and
519 Broadway, 5th Floor
New York NY 10012

www.rylandpeters.com

Text © Fiona Beckett, Maxine Clark, Clare Ferguson,
Silvana Franca, Liz Franklin, Tonia George, Brian
Glover, Amanda Grant, Rachael Anne Hill, Caroline
Marson, Louise Pickford, Lindy Wildsmith and
Ryland Peters & Small 2014

Design and photographs © Ryland Peters & Small
2014

ISBN: 978-1-84975-501-6

10 9 8 7 6 5 4 3 2 1

A CIP record for this book is available from
the British Library.

US Library of Congress Cataloging-in-Publication
data has been applied for.

Printed and bound in China

notes:

• All spoon measurements are level, unless
otherwise specified.
• All eggs are medium UK/large US, unless
otherwise specified. Recipes containing raw or
partially cooked egg should not be served to the
very young, very old, anyone with a compromised
immune system or pregnant women.

contents

introduction

For those of us who lead busy lives but still want
to eat healthy and fresh food, pasta is often the
first choice – it's one of the few dishes that can be
ready to eat within half an hour of getting home.
Pasta makes such ideal everyday food, not only
because it's so quick and easy, but also because
it can be incredibly varied. In this book you'll find
a fantastic range of homemade sauces, all using
readily available ingredients. Pasta goes with
almost everything; meat, seafood, vegetables,
cheese – the list is endless. Many of the sauces in
this book can be made in the time it takes to boil
the pasta, while others can be prepared ahead
of time and reheated, making life even easier.

Dried, fresh and filled pasta weights are given
on page 140. Fresh pasta is only recommended
when you want ready-stuffed shapes. A simple
sauce can go really well with fresh shapes, but in
general it is best to buy good-quality dried pasta,
made with 100 per cent durum wheat. It cooks
to a firm and springy bite (known in Italian as
al dente), comes in a huge range of shapes and
sizes, and is very convenient to buy and store.
That said, if you have a little more time and energy
to spare, then making your own pasta noodles
is surprisingly easy and satisfying (see pages
132–139) and it will never fail to impress!

classic ingredients

Simple Italian ingredients, such as olive oil, tomatoes and Parmesan are essential to most pasta dishes – choose carefully and buy the best quality foods you can afford and the flavour of your cooking will benefit. Remember, a flavourless tomato will give you a flavourless pasta sauce!

Olive oil

Using a good quality olive oil can make all the difference to the flavour of a pasta dish. Olive oil should be used within 18 months of production, because it will turn rancid, especially when exposed to light and heat. Either buy it in a can or store the bottle in a cool dark place and decant it into a stainless steel or ceramic pourer for regular kitchen and table use.

Tomatoes

It's hard to imagine cooking without tomatoes, whether raw, cooked, as a paste, chopped and canned, or as a sauce. Of course, everyone says that tomatoes don't taste the way they used to. They probably don't, because modern farming methods require varieties that can be picked, packed, transported and sold without damage. That doesn't necessarily go hand-in-hand with flavour. However, it is still possible to find tomatoes with that real old-fashioned flavour. Farmers' markets are the best source, and they're also sold in organic food stores and special sections in some supermarkets.

Look for the delicious heirloom varieties, or those based on the traditional Italian plum tomato or the French Marmande, with its furrowed skin. Mini tomatoes seem to have more flavour, and even regular tomatoes have more taste if they're left to ripen on the vine.

When choosing tomatoes, make sure they are firm to the touch and have a light bloom on the skin – and don't forget to smell them! Discover where they were grown and, whenever possible, buy tomatoes ripened in the sun and not forced out of season.

Although we tend to associate beef and plum tomatoes with Italy, they are not necessarily a good choice in other parts of the world, where they can often be pithy and flavourless. Put them and vine tomatoes through this same test – all are more expensive, but don't necessarily taste better.

Good quality Italian canned peeled tomatoes 'pellati', (whole or 'fillets') are a good option for cooked tomato sauces as you can be sure they are sun-ripened and flavoursome.

Grating cheeses

The king of grating cheeses is undoubtedly Parmesan though the term tends to be used of any cheese made in a similar crystalline, crumbly style. True Parmesan is labelled as Parmigiano-Reggiano and comes from the Emilia-Romagna region of Italy around the cities of Parma and Modena, where it is aged for up to 4 years (1–2 years is more common). Grana Padano, which looks very similar, is usually younger and can come from anywhere in Italy. Other cheeses that grate well include Pecorino Romano which is made from sheeps' milk and has a tangy flavour. You could also try Swiss Sbrinz, and Vella Dry Jack from California.

When serving pasta, have a small block of Parmesan with a fine grater and pass them around the table so everyone can grate their own. The only time Parmesan should not be offered is if the sauce is fish or seafood. It just doesn't go, and you would certainly never see it on an Italian table. That said, if the seafood or fish sauce is creamy, a grating of Parmesan can sometimes work.

If you're adding cheese to a sauce, take the sauce off the heat first before adding it bit by bit until it has melted. If necessary, reheat the sauce just enough to melt the cheese completely. Cheese cooked too long or at too high a temperature will become rubbery and stringy.

making the most of herbs

Fresh and dried herbs add their own unique character of flavour and fragrance to food and are widely used in Italian pasta dishes. Some herbs can be quite overpowering if used in a heavy-handed way, so getting to know them a little better will help you to get the best out of them.

A herb's aroma and flavour comes from the volatile oils stored in the leaves, flowers and stems. As a rule of thumb, woody herbs, such as bay and sage, tend to stand up to longer cooking and can be added at the beginning of cooking. Those with soft, delicate leave or fronds, such as basil, coriander and dill, are a little more sensitive and are best added towards the end of cooking time. Here is a little background on some of the herbs most commonly used in classic Italian cooking and in the recipes with a more modern twist you'll find in this book.

Basil Basil takes its name from the Greek basileus, meaning 'king'. It is actually native to India, where it is sacred and known as 'tulsi'. It was first brought to Egypt around 3000 years ago, then on to Rome and so to all parts of southern Europe. These days the common basil we know as sweet or Italian basil grows wherever the climate suits. Many cooks have a rule that basil must only be torn, not cut as metal reacts with the plant juices, turning the cut edges black and bitter.

Pesto sauce relies almost entirely on the glorious flavour of basil. Though less traditional, coriander (see below) can also be used – see pages 29–30) for some simple **Homemade Pestos**.

Oregano Oregano is a woody perennial, and the hotter the sun the stronger the flavour. Italians use the flower heads just before they bloom as well as the leaves to flavour dishes. The many wild species of oregano are known collectively as 'rigani', which grow wild on hillsides and mountains throughout Greece. It is an essential ingredient in Italian cooking – where would they be without it for tomato sauces ? Try the **Quick Neapolitan Tomato Sauce** on page 18.

Flat-leaf parsley Flat leaf parsley (or French, Italian or Continental parsley, as it's often called) is essential to many traditional flavouring mixtures, including the Italian gremolata – a mix of parsley, chopped garlic and lemon zest, which is sprinkled over finished dishes. It is an essential component of simple seafood pasta sauces, such as **Baby Clam Sauce** (see page 37).

Bay leaves The bay tree was originally a wild plant of the Mediterranean, where it still thrives today. Greek and Roman heroes were crowned with wreaths of bay leaves as a symbol of excellence. When you crush the leaves, the aromas range from grassy and floral to bitter – as a flavouring herb, they stand up to long cooking, which brings out their sweet mellowness. The subtle flavour of bay is particular welcome in a classic **Bolognese Sauce** (see page 26).

Rosemary Rosemary has been a culinary and medicinal herb since ancient Greek and Roman times. Apart from the classic partnerships with roast lamb or monkfish, the leaves are also capable of delivering some delicious flavours to meat sauces and stands up well to the other robust flavours in the **Pork and Lemon Ragu** on page 99.

Sage From the Latin word salvere meaning 'to save', sage is a highly valued medicinal herb. It is known as the 'herb of the heart' and chewing the leaves is said to make teeth white and shiny. It is a popular herb in many regions of Italy and its pungent robustness adds a new dimension to buttery dishes in particular. A **Foaming Sage Butter** (see page 38) is often served with filled ravioli and gnocchi.

Thyme Thyme from the Greek thymos – 'to perfume' – has so many varieties, full of character and all with their own subtle aroma and flavour.

The ancient Egyptians and Greeks knew the powerful antiseptic and preservative qualities of thyme. Roman cooks used it to preserve their meat: those strong antiseptic qualities delayed spoiling. Thyme adds a unusual and delicious note to the **Chilli Tuna Tartare** pasta on page 72.

Coriander Coriander is mentioned in the Bible and in Sanskrit texts and was found in Egyptian tombs in seed form. It was brought to Europe by late bronze-age nomads, while the Spaniards carried it to Mexico and Peru, where it became a partner to their much-loved chilli. The Arab-influenced Italian dish, **Calabrese and Broccoli Arabesque** (see page 51) showcases it's unique flavour.

Mint Mint was introduced to Europe by the Romans and has remained the most popular herb in the world. Peppermint tea of course is the drink of choice throughout the Middle East as it is as stimulating as coffee. It's refreshing flavour can cut through a creamy pasta sauce and it works particularly well with lemon – try the **Courgette, Mint, Lemon and Cream sauce** on page 59.

Dill Dill started out in the Middle East in biblical times. It migrated with travellers into Europe, North and South America, further east into Asia as well as north to Scandinavia. Its name comes appropriately from the old Norse word dylla meaning 'to lull'. The leaves are sweet with hints of

anise that aren't as strong as fennel, but similar to caraway in taste. It is used extensively in Scandinavian cooking with fish, eggs and potatoes and it works very well with richer seafood pasta dishes such as the **Lobster Sauce** on page 64.

Chopping herbs

• Use a very sharp blade for chopping herbs, so the leaves don't lose all their flavour into your chopping board.
• A mezzaluna (see photo centre right) is easy to use and ideal for coarsely chopping herbs – it has a curved double-handled blade, which you rock from side to side over the leaves.
• When using a knife, wrap the herbs into a tight bunch with your fingers, then chop with the blade close to your fingers, and angled away from you.
• To chop even finer, bunch the leaves back together again, and chop using the knife as a pivot.
• Chopping leaves in a food processor is fine if you're adding or beginning with other ingredients, otherwise it's much better to use a large cook's knife. If you do need to use a food processor use the pulse button to give you more control.
• When using woody herbs or herbs with lots of stalk, strip the leaves off first.
• Dry leaves are better to work with, so after washing, drain well and leave on paper towels for 20 minutes to air dry. Stronger leaves can be dried in a salad spinner without bruising.

enjoying wine with pasta

With a simple, everyday dish like pasta, why not have a simple, everyday wine? Italian whites and reds are the natural choice — especially as Italy now offers so many exciting, well-priced wines. Those made elsewhere using Italian grape varieties — Sangiovese, Barbera and so on — also feel comfortingly authentic. But there are other possibilities.

Vegetable-based

Spinach and ricotta Stick to crisp, dry whites — Frascati, Soave or Pinot Grigio from Italy, or any light Chardonnay.

Roasted vegetables with garlic Go for fruity whites (Cote de Rhone or Languedoc blends, Californian Fume Blanc, Australian Verdelho) or light juicy reds such as inexpensive New World Pinot Noir.

Basil pesto Whites work better than reds here. Choose something like Lugana, Vernacchia di San Gimignano or Soave from Italy, Alsace Pinot Blanc or unoaked New World Chardonnay.

Fresh tomato and basil Fresh Italian whites such as Pinot Grigio or Lugana are excellent — but so is Sauvignon Blanc from the Loire, Chile or New Zealand.

Rich tomato sauce You'd get by with a white wine like Pinot Grigio, but reds make a happier marriage. Maybe a young Chianti (or New World Sangiovese); Barbera from Italy, California or Australia; or a sunbaked southern Italian like Primitivo and its American 'cousin', Zinfandel.

Mushrooms Take your pick between crisp white and round red. In the white camp, Frascati, Orvieto and unoaked Chardonnay. In the red, Dolcetto d'Alba, Chilean Merlot and New World Pinot Noir.

Sage butter The strong flavour of sage tastes just right with a restrained Sauvignon Blanc — one that's pungent and grassy, not laden with tropical fruit. Try a north-eastern Italian version for authenticity, or a Sancerre or Pouilly-Fumé from the Loire.

Creamy

Carbonara Counter the richness of eggs, cream, ham and Parmesan with a fairly crisp white wine. Northern Italians like Pinot Grigio and Gavi perform well, as does Sardinian Vermentino or any light Chardonnay.

Cheese Whether it's pasta with four cheeses or macaroni cheese, you'll need one of the crisp whites unless you prefer a light red like a simple young Chianti from Tuscany or Barbera from northern Italy.

Meat

Bolognese and ragu Red, for sure, and middleweight, such as Chianti Classico or any Sangiovese; Valpolicella Ripasso or a good New World Merlot.

Spicy sausage Big flavours cry out for a rich red with plenty of ripeness to cope with the heat. Consider Australian Grenache-Shiraz blends, Zinfandel from Chile or California, or anything from Italy's deep south (such as Salice Salentino).

Fish

Seafood (clams, mussels) Stick with the Italian 'Vs' — Verdicchio, Vernaccia di San Gimignano or Sardinia's Vermentino. Otherwise, the crispest, driest white you can find. A light Chardonnay would work.

Salmon or smoked salmon Chardonnay, unoaked or lightly oaked (Burgundy, northern Italy, Chile, New Zealand) is pretty unbeatable.

Puttanesca Go for the contrast of a cooling, neutral white like Frascati or Pinot Grigio, or fight back with a fruity, characterful red — one from Sicily, perhaps, a young Primitivo or a not-too-full-bodied Californian or smooth Chilean Zinfandel.

Classic pasta sauces have their origins in the traditional cooking of regional Italy. Some of them are uniquely linked to one region, while some feature in the cooking of many regions and there are many versions of the same recipe.

the classics

This useful base sauce begins with a classic battuto (chopping) of carrot, onion and celery, used often in Italian cooking. This sauce originates from Bologna and is more substantial and has a stronger flavour than the Neapolitan recipe on page 18. It is also the best recipe for non-plum tomatoes, because the vegetable base gives the extra flavour that other tomato varieties lack. Serve it with any pasta shape, freshly chopped basil and plenty of freshly grated Parmesan.

basic tomato sauce

1 kg/2 lbs fresh tomatoes

2 tablespoons unsalted butter

2 tablespoons olive oil

1 small celery stalk, finely chopped

1 small carrot, finely chopped

1 small onion, finely chopped

a small bunch of basil, chopped

sea salt and freshly ground black pepper

To serve

freshly cooked pasta of your choice (see page 140)

a handful of fresh basil leaves, torn or finely chopped

extra virgin olive oil

freshly grated Parmesan

Serves 4–6

To prepare the tomatoes, cut a cross in the base of each one, squeeze out the seeds and discard them.

Heat the butter and olive oil in a heavy-based saucepan over high heat. When it starts to bubble, add the celery, carrot, onion, herbs and tomatoes. Stir quickly in the hot fat for a few minutes, then lower the heat, cover and simmer for 1 hour. Stir from time to time, adding a little water as the tomatoes reduce.

Push the sauce though a mouli (food mill) or sieve/strainer. Add salt and pepper to taste.

Toss the sauce through the pasta, then add the Parmesan and sprinkle with torn or chopped basil and drizzle with olive oil. Serve a dish of Parmesan separately for people to help themselves.

Notes

When plum tomatoes are out of season, Italian cooks use pellati (canned tomatoes). Make sure you use a good Italian brand – buy whole or fillets, rather than chopped, to ensure quality.

quick Neapolitan tomato sauce

1 kg/2 lbs canned plum tomatoes, deseeded, drained (reserve the juice) and chopped

5 tablespoons olive oil

4 garlic cloves

your choice of:
1 small piece of fresh red chilli, ½ cinnamon stick, ½ teaspoon dried oregano, or a bunch of fresh herbs, such as basil

sea salt and freshly ground black pepper

To serve

freshly cooked pasta of your choice (see page 140)

freshly grated Parmesan

a handful of fresh herbs, torn or finely chopped

extra virgin olive oil

Serves 4–6

This classic tomato sauce comes originally from Campania, the region around Naples. The great nineteenth-century Italian food writer, Pellegrino Artusi, believed it to be beneficial to the digestive system; it certainly goes down a treat. It is made simply with tomatoes, olive oil, garlic and the flavouring of your choice. You can use Italian canned plum tomatoes, making it a handy standby.

Put the prepared tomatoes, oil and garlic in a heavy-based saucepan. Add your choice of the chilli, cinnamon and dried or fresh herbs. Cover and simmer over low heat for 30 minutes, or until the tomatoes are reduced to a creamy mass.

Stir from time to time to stop the sauce sticking to the bottom of the pan. Add a little of the reserved tomato juice whenever necessary to keep the sauce moist. Discard the garlic and chilli, cinnamon or herbs. Mash the sauce with a potato masher. If using fresh herbs, it may be necessary to purée the sauce in a blender. Taste and adjust the seasoning with salt and freshly ground black pepper.

Pour the sauce over the pasta, top with the Parmesan, sprinkle with fresh herbs, then serve at once with extra cheese and olive oil for drizzling.

Variations
Chop a mozzarella ball into small cubes and stir through the pasta sauce before serving. Add a handful of torn basil leaves to the bowl and stir well before serving.

There are few dishes more pure than a sauce made of fresh tomatoes enhanced with a little garlic, chilli, olive oil and herbs. Here the tomatoes are roasted first to give them a really sweet flavour. This versatile tomato sauce can be served with spaghetti, as part of vegetable lasagne, or as a pizza topping, as well as providing the base for soups or stews.

spicy roasted tomato sauce

1 kg/2 lbs vine-ripened tomatoes, roughly chopped

2 tablespoons olive oil

2 garlic cloves, crushed

grated zest of 1 unwaxed lemon

a pinch of dried chilli flakes/hot red pepper flakes

2 tablespoons chopped fresh basil

sea salt and freshly ground black pepper

freshly cooked pasta of your choice (see page 140) to serve

Serves 4

Preheat the oven to 230°C (450°F) Gas 8.

Put the tomatoes, olive oil, garlic, lemon zest, chilli flakes and seasoning in a roasting pan in a single layer. Toss well. Roast for 45 minutes, or until the tomatoes are browned and the juices reduced to a glaze.

Transfer the tomatoes and all the pan juices to a deep bowl, add the basil and, using a hand blender, purée until smooth. Season to taste. Serve hot with pasta or leave to cool and freeze in a plastic container to use another time.

Note During the summer months, when tomatoes are plentiful and at their best, make up several quantities of this sauce and freeze for use in the winter.

If you like spicy and simple food, this is for you. It is a typical dish of the mountainous Abruzzo region, where long snowy winters have inspired all kinds of warming specialities popular with the skiers who flock there. Local fiery chillies, or diavolini (little devils) as they are called, are added to many of the region's dishes, salami and cured meats. Make this dressing swiftly, cook the pasta al dente, use the best-quality ingredients and serve straight away. Serve as a starter/appetizer until you become a connoisseur.

simple garlic and chilli sauce

150 ml/⅔ cup extra virgin olive oil

4 garlic cloves, peeled but whole

1 small to medium dried chilli (to taste), finely chopped

2 handfuls of flat-leaf parsley, finely chopped

To serve

freshly cooked pasta of your choice (see page 140)

freshly grated Parmesan (optional)

Serves 4

While the pasta is boiling, slowly heat the olive oil in a frying pan/skillet with the garlic and chilli. When the garlic turns golden, discard it. Drain the pasta, then return it to the saucepan. Add the hot flavoured oil, chilli pieces and chopped parsley and stir well. Serve at once, with Parmesan, if using.

Variation

Arrabbiata For spice lovers, this is a tomato-based version of the first recipe. The word arrabbiata means 'rabid' and is used in Italian to mean 'angry'. It is a popular dish in Rome and generally made on demand in simple eateries. Use the tomato sauce recipe on page 18 (Quick Neapolitan Tomato Sauce), but double the amount of garlic and chillies. Add 2 handfuls of flat-leaf parsley, finely chopped, at the end.

1 tablespoon olive oil

1 tablespoon unsalted butter

1 small carrot, finely chopped

1 small celery stalk, finely chopped

1 small onion, finely chopped.

100 g/4 oz pancetta or streaky bacon, minced/ground

500 g/1 lb 2 oz lean minced/ground steak

2 tablespoons white wine

375 ml/1½ cups full-fat milk, or enough to cover the meat

1½ tablespoons tomato purée/paste

freshly grated nutmeg, to taste

250–500 ml/1–2 cups warm stock or water, as required

sea salt and freshly ground black pepper

To serve

freshly cooked pasta of your choice (see page 140)

50 g/¼ cup freshly grated Parmesan, plus extra to taste

3 tablespoons freshly chopped flat-leaf parsley

2 tablespoons unsalted butter

Serves 4–6

ragù meat sauce

In Bologna in Northern Italy, the meat sauce that is served is called ragù (not Bolognese sauce) and it is enjoyed with tagliatelle or rigatoni, but never with spaghetti! They do have a salsa bolognese (Bolognese sauce), but it is made with oranges and Marsala wine and served with duck. Here is an authentic and delicious recipe for a Bolognese-style ragù which is both rich and satisfying.

Heat the oil and butter in a heavy-based saucepan over medium heat. Add the chopped carrot, celery, onion and pancetta and cook until transparent. Increase the heat, add the meat and fry until browned. Add the wine and let it bubble until it has evaporated.

Lower the heat, add enough milk to cover the meat, then add the tomato purée/paste and a little nutmeg. Cook rapidly until the milk has reduced by at least half. Lower the heat, top up with enough warm stock or water to cover the meat, stir, cover with a lid and simmer for at least 1 hour. Stir from time to time.

Add salt and pepper to taste, then set aside to rest overnight to develop the flavours.

When ready to serve, reheat the sauce and add to the pasta. Stir in the cheese, parsley and butter and serve with extra cheese.

bolognese sauce

125 g/5 oz smoked pancetta, diced

2 tablespoons olive oil

1 large onion, finely chopped

2 garlic cloves, finely chopped

1 tablespoon chopped fresh thyme

750 g/1 lb 10 oz minced/
ground beef

50 g/2 oz chicken livers, diced

300 ml/1¼ cups red wine

2 x 400-g/14-oz cans chopped
tomatoes

2 tablespoons tomato purée/paste

a pinch of sugar

2 fresh bay leaves (or 1 dried)

sea salt and freshly ground
black pepper

To serve

freshly cooked pasta of your
choice (see page 140)

freshly grated Parmesan

Serves 4–6

Spaghetti bolognese must be the original fusion dish, an invention as British as roast beef! That said, it still deserves a place in your pasta sauce repetoire and the addition of chicken livers adds a great depth of flavour to this foolproof recipe. Serve over freshly cooked spaghetti with plenty of freshly grated Parmesan.

Heat a saucepan and dry-fry the pancetta for 3–4 minutes, or until browned and the fat is rendered into the pan. Remove from the pan with a slotted spoon and set aside.

Add the olive oil to the same pan and gently fry the onion, garlic and thyme for 10 minutes, or until softened. Increase the heat, add the beef and chicken livers and stir-fry for 5 minutes, or until browned.

Add the wine and bring to the boil, then stir in the canned tomatoes, tomato purée/paste, sugar, bay leaves, fried pancetta and seasoning. Cover and simmer over low heat for 1–1½ hours, or until the sauce has thickened. Discard the bay leaves and season to taste. Serve with with pasta and plenty of Parmesan.

homemade pestos

Homemade pesto not only looks and smells better than a pesto from a jar – it also tastes better! Pestos are perfect for stirring into pasta, drizzling on pizza or as a topping for grilled fish or chicken. Put the pestos in a screw-top jar, add a thin layer of oil and refrigerate for up to a week. Each recipe here makes sufficient for 4–6 servings.

classic basil pesto

A lot of precious leaves are needed to make up this sauce, but it is well worth the indulgence. Serve with pasta, spread on toasts and pizza, or add to mashed potatoes and soups.

50 g/2 oz fresh basil leaves
1 large garlic clove, crushed
25 g/¼ cup pine nuts, toasted
5–6 tablespoons extra virgin olive oil
a pinch of sea salt
30 g/1 oz Parmesan or Pecorino Romano, finely grated

Put the basil, garlic, pine nuts, olive oil and salt in a mini food processor. Blend until smooth, then stir in the grated cheese.

coriander, chilli and peanut pesto

This hot and spicy pesto is perfect with vegetable and seafood stir-fries, stirred through pasta or noodles and served as a dip for crudités.

100 g/1 cup roasted and salted peanuts
1 garlic clove, crushed
1 red or green fresh chilli, deseeded and chopped
20 g/1 oz fresh coriander/cilantro leaves
finely grated zest of 1 unwaxed lime
100 ml/⅓ cup groundnut or sunflower oil
sea salt and freshly ground black pepper

Put the peanuts, garlic and chilli in the bowl of a mini food processor. Blend, then add the coriander/ cilantro and lime zest, season generously and pulse to form a coarse mix. Allow the motor to run and then, in a steady flow, add the groundnut oil to form a smooth paste. Taste and season as necessary.

red pepper and walnut pesto

Serve this warm as a dip for crudités, stirred into cooked pasta, spooned over grilled halloumi cheese or as a sauce with grilled lamb or steak.

2 chargrilled red (bell) peppers
55 g/½ cup walnut pieces, toasted
3 spring onions/scallions, chopped
1 garlic clove, crushed
2 tablespoons chopped fresh parsley
4–5 tablespoons extra virgin olive oil
sea salt and freshly ground black pepper

Put all the ingredients in a mini food processor and blitz until smooth. Taste and season as necessary.

Variation If you have time, roast your own red peppers; place under a preheated high grill/broiler until the skins are blackened on all sides. Remove and put in a plastic bag for 10 minutes, then slip off the skins.

artichoke and almond pesto

This has a lovely creamy texture and subtle flavour. Add to pasta or spread onto warm ciabatta toasts, or serve as a dip with grissini (bread sticks). Marinated artichoke hearts can be found loose at deli counters or in jars in the Italian section of supermarkets.

4–6 roasted and marinated artichokes hearts, drained
100 g/1 cup almonds, toasted (see Mint, Ginger and Almond Pesto, right)
2 tablespoons chopped fresh basil
1 garlic clove, crushed
4 tablespoons extra virgin olive oil
30 g/1 oz Parmesan, finely grated
sea salt and freshly ground black pepper

Put the artichokes, almonds, basil and garlic in a mini food processor. Blitz until the mixture looks like coarse meal. Add the oil in a thin stream with the motor running to form a smooth paste. Transfer the purée to a bowl and stir in the Parmesan. Taste and season as necessary.

broccoli, parmesan and basil pesto

This is a wonderfully vibrant green pesto and is delicious tossed through pasta, spread onto toast or served as a warm dip.

125 g/5 oz broccoli florets
25 g/¼ cup pine nuts, toasted
1 large garlic clove, crushed
1 fresh red chilli, deseeded and finely chopped
3 tablespoons extra virgin olive oil
55 g/2 oz Parmesan, finely grated
freshly squeezed juice of ½ a lemon
sea salt and freshly ground black pepper

Cook the broccoli in a pan of boiling salted water until tender, about 6–7 minutes. Drain. Meanwhile, put the pine nuts, garlic and chilli in a mini food processor and pulse to form a coarse mix. Add the broccoli and olive oil and pulse until the mixture is smooth. Add the Parmesan and lemon juice and pulse again. Taste and season as necessary.

mint, ginger and almond pesto

This is lovely spooned over grilled fish or vegetables, added to clear vegetable soup or tossed into cooked noodles. Toasting the almonds gives the pesto a more intense flavour. Look out for packets of pre-toasted almonds or toast them yourself in the oven for 5–6 minutes at 200°C (400°F) Gas 6. Keep an eye on them as they burn quickly.

2-cm/1-inch piece of fresh ginger root, peeled and grated
20 g/1 oz fresh mint leaves
8 tablespoons vegetable oil
2 tablespoons light soy sauce
1 tablespoon freshly squeezed lime juice
1 garlic clove, crushed
100 g/½ cup almonds, toasted

Put all the ingredients in the bowl of a mini food processor and blitz until smooth.

olive oil, for cooking

1 garlic clove, peeled and left whole

1 small piece of dried chilli, finely chopped (to taste)

1 x 50-g/2-oz can anchovy fillets, drained and mashed

2 x 400-g/14-oz cans plum tomatoes, drained (reserve the juice), deseeded and chopped

5 tablespoons capers (if salted, rinse well and pat dry with paper towels)

100 g/¾ cup black olives

freshly ground black pepper

To serve

freshly cooked pasta of your choice (see page 140)

a handful of fresh flat-leaf parsley, finely chopped

extra virgin olive oil

Serves 4–6

puttanesca sauce

This is from Campania, from the island of Ischia. Suffice to say, the combination of the local ingredients — olive oil, garlic, chillies, anchovies, tomatoes, olives and capers — packs a real punch.

Cover the base of a medium saucepan with olive oil. Add the garlic and chilli and set over low heat. Remove the garlic clove as soon as it starts to turn golden.

Add the mashed anchovy, chopped tomatoes, capers, olives and plenty of black pepper. Stir and continue cooking until the sauce has reduced and darkened in colour, about 20–30 minutes. If the sauce starts to dry out too much, stir in a little of the reserved tomato juice.

Add the sauce to the freshly cooked pasta and stir well. Add the parsley and a drizzle of oil and serve.

2 whole eggs

5 egg yolks

2 tablespoons unsalted butter

125 ml/½ cup single/light cream

6 tablespoons freshly grated
Parmesan

200 g/7 oz pancetta or bacon

olive oil, for frying

1 garlic clove, crushed

freshly ground black pepper

To serve

freshly cooked pasta of your
choice (see page 140)

freshly grated Parmesan cheese

freshly ground black pepper

Serves 4–6

carbonara sauce

**Crisp, garlic-scented bacon with a stream of creamy fresh eggs
setting in the warm pasta, fragrant with the scent of freshly grated
Parmesan. It is easy to understand why this is a enduringly popular
pasta sauce, and one of the speciality dishes found in every simple
eatery in Rome.**

Put the eggs and egg yolks in a bowl and mix lightly with a fork. Add
the butter, cream, grated Parmesan and lots of black pepper. Let stand
without mixing.

Chop the pancetta into slivers. Cover the base of a medium frying
pan/skillet with olive oil and heat through. When it starts to haze, add
the pancetta. When the fat starts to run, add the crushed garlic and stir
well. Continue frying until the pancetta becomes crisp and golden.

Add the pancetta and pan juices to the freshly cooked pasta and mix
vigorously. Beat the egg mixture lightly with a fork and pour over the
pasta. Mix well and serve at once with extra cheese and plenty of freshly
ground black pepper – the butter will melt and the eggs will cook in the
heat of the pasta.

Spaghettini with clams is typical of the regional cuisine of almost every coastal area in Italy, but is most often associated with the Amalfi coast, in particular the picturesque town of Positano and the islands of Ischia and Capri. It is served in two versions – bianco (oil, garlic and parsley) or al pomodoro (tomato sauce).

baby clam sauce

1 kg/2 lbs small fresh clams, in their shells

125–150 ml/½–⅔ cup olive oil

1 garlic clove, peeled but whole

a piece of dried chilli

2 handfuls of fresh flat-leaf parsley, finely chopped

To serve

freshly cooked pasta of your choice (see page 140)

freshly ground black pepper

a handful of fresh flat-leaf parsley, roughly chopped

extra virgin olive oil

Serves 4–6

Wash the clams in plenty of running water until not a trace of sand is left. Drain well. Put them in a heavy-based saucepan over high heat. Cover with a lid and shake the pan until all the clams have opened. Strain off the liquid, pour it through a fine sieve/strainer and reserve. Reduce if necessary.

Heat the olive oil in a large saucepan, add the garlic and chilli and heat through gently. When the garlic starts to turn golden, discard it and the chilli. Add the clams to the pan, together with their strained cooking liquid. Add the parsley and cook gently for a minute or two for the flavours to blend.

Add the clams to the freshly cooked pasta and mix well. Tip onto a large serving plate and top with lots of black pepper, some more parsley and olive oil. Serve at once.

Variation

Spaghettini con le vongole al pomodoro (with tomatoes) Skin, deseed and chop 500 g/2 lbs plum tomatoes, then add to the oil at the same time as the garlic and chilli. Cook over low heat for 20–30 minutes until reduced to a creamy mass. Add the clams and the strained juices and cook for a minute or so for the flavours to blend. Add the parsley and proceed as in the main recipe.

foaming sage butter

125 g/1 stick unsalted butter

2 tablespoons chopped fresh sage

2 garlic cloves, crushed

sea salt and freshly ground
black pepper

Serves 2

This is so simple, yet totally delicious – melted butter is sautéed until golden and nutty then mixed with fresh sage leaves and a little crushed garlic. It is particularly good with pumpkin-filled ravioli, spinach and ricotta gnocchi, or simply with plain pasta noodles.

Melt the butter in a small frying pan/skillet, then cook over medium heat for 3–4 minutes until it turns golden brown. Remove the pan from the heat and add the sage leaves, garlic and a little seasoning. Leave to sizzle in the butter for 30 seconds until fragrant. Serve immediately.

There are an infinite number of delicious pasta dishes that can be made with vegetables. They can be cooked from scratch with tomatoes, or fried in flavoured oils, roasted or cooked gently in melted butter and herbs.

vegetables

primavera

In Italy every morning barring Sunday you will find streets and squares crammed with market stalls, spilling over with fresh vegetables picked that morning and proudly labelled nostrani (home produce). There is nothing like a vegetable grown in your own soil, then picked, cooked and eaten on the same day. Seeking out a farmers' market near you, buy seasonally and reinvent this simple recipe as the crops change.

olive oil, for cooking

1 onion, finely chopped

2 tablespoons white wine

500 g/1 lb 2 oz green vegetables, such as green beans, asparagus, peas, broad beans/fava or a mixture (shelled weight)

400 g/14 oz ripe tomatoes, skinned, deseeded and chopped

a handful of fresh mint, finely chopped

a handful of fresh basil, finely chopped

3 tablespoons freshly grated Parmesan

80 g/3 oz Parma ham cut into strips (optional)

sea salt and freshly ground black pepper

To serve

freshly cooked pasta of your choice (see page 140)

basil leaves

Serves 4

If using asparagus or green beans, cut them into short lengths. Cover the base of a frying pan/skillet with olive oil and heat gently. Add the onion and fry gently until softened and translucent. Add the wine and let bubble until evaporated. Stir in the green vegetables and tomatoes, then add salt and pepper to taste. Stir again, cover with a lid and cook for 10–20 minutes or until tender. Stir in the herbs, then taste again for seasoning.

Add the sauce to the freshly cooked pasta, then add the grated Parmesan and strips of Parma ham, if using. Stir well and serve topped with basil leaves.

Variations

Vary the vegetables and herbs according to season. Try young carrots with spring cabbage, 1 teaspoon crushed juniper berries and 1 teaspoon chopped thyme.

Omit the Parma ham and use a handful of sun-dried tomatoes, thinly sliced, 1½ tablespoons capers and 1½ tablespoons black olives.

Omit the Parma ham and add 1 tablespoon finely chopped anchovies, finely chopped zest of 1 small unwaxed lemon and a handful of fresh flat-leaf parsley, finely chopped.

roasted vegetables with capers and cherry tomatoes

1 small aubergine/eggplant

1 red (bell) pepper, halved and deseeded

1 yellow (bell) pepper, halved and deseeded

3 small courgettes/zucchini

2 leeks, split and well washed

1½ tablespoons finely chopped fresh rosemary needles

2 garlic cloves, finely chopped

2 tablespoons olive oil

1–2 tablespoons capers, rinsed and drained

about 10 cherry tomatoes

To serve

freshly cooked pasta of your choice (see page 140)

extra virgin olive oil

6 sprigs of fresh rosemary

freshly grated Parmesan

Serves 4

When choosing peppers, aubergines, tomatoes and the like, squeeze them lightly to ensure the flesh is firm. Don't worry if they're funny shapes, it's more important that they are fresh – even better if they have a bloom to them. When buying leeks, make sure you aren't paying a premium for a bunch of leaves and you have a good proportion of white trunk, the really tender, sweet part. Don't be put off by the leaves, however – providing they are fresh, just cut them off and put them in the stockpot. Italians don't waste a thing and neither should any good cook.

Preheat the oven to 200°C (400°F) Gas 6.

Cut the aubergine/eggplants, (bell) peppers, courgettes/zucchini and leeks into bite-size pieces, about 2 cm/1-inch square, and arrange in a single layer in a roasting pan. Add the rosemary, garlic and olive oil and mix well with your hands. Cover with foil, transfer to the preheated oven and roast for 20–30 minutes until tender. Remove and discard the foil, add the capers and cherry tomatoes, stir well and roast for a further 10 minutes.

Add the roasted vegetables to the freshly cooked pasta, stir well and spread out on a serving plate. Sprinkle with oil and rosemary and serve with grated Parmesan.

uncooked pasta of your choice
(see page 120)

300 g/10 oz broccoli florets

1 tablespoon olive oil

2 garlic cloves, crushed

½ teaspoon dried chilli/hot red
pepper flakes

3 anchovy fillets, roughly chopped

100 g/½ cup crème fraîche

sea salt and freshly ground
black pepper

To serve

freshly grated Parmesan

Serves 2

You can save time and washing up here by cooking the broccoli in the same pan as the pasta. If it's in season, use purple sprouting broccoli. Trim the fiborous ends, then slice into 1-cm/½-inch lengths, dividing the florets into bite-size pieces. The anchovy is already very salty, so it's best to taste a forkful before adding any more salt.

broccoli, anchovy, parmesan and crème fraîche

Bring a large saucepan of salted water to the boil. Add the pasta, cover with a lid and bring back to the boil. Remove the lid, stir the pasta and cook according to the packet instructions. Add the broccoli to the pasta 3–4 minutes before the end of cooking. Drain the pasta and the broccoli well and reserve a little of the cooking water.

Wipe out the pan and add the olive oil. Cook the garlic, chilli flakes and anchovies over low heat for about 2 minutes. Add the crème fraîche, season with a little pepper and bring to the boil. Return the cooked broccoli and pasta to the pan, adding a little of the reserved pasta cooking water if necessary to thin the sauce down. Season to taste with black pepper.

Divide the pasta between serving bowls and serve immediately, sprinkled with Parmesan.

150 ml/⅔ cup vegetable stock

175 g/1½ cups trimmed and chopped asparagus

200 g/3 cups sliced button mushrooms

400-g/14-oz can artichoke hearts, drained and halved

150 g/1 cup chopped extra-lean cooked ham

Light pesto

4 garlic cloves, crushed

8 tablespoons chopped fresh basil leaves

8 tablespoons half-fat crème fraîche

4 tablespoons freshly grated Parmesan

freshly ground black pepper

To serve

freshly cooked pasta of your choice (see page 140)

2 tablespoons shredded fresh basil leaves

freshly shaved Parmesan

Serves 4

creamy artichoke, asparagus and ham sauce

The pine nuts and olive oil traditionally used in pesto make it high in fat. The combination of garlic, fresh basil and half-fat crème fraîche used in this recipe creates a healthier, low-fat version while still packing a mean-tasting punch!

Put the stock and asparagus in a saucepan. Bring to the boil, reduce the heat, cover and simmer for 2 minutes. Add the mushrooms and simmer for a further 2 minutes, until the asparagus is just tender. Drain and set aside.

To make the pesto, put the garlic, basil, crème fraîche, Parmesan and black pepper in a food processor or blender. Process for a few seconds, until smooth. Alternatively, finely chop the basil and mix all the ingredients together in a bowl.

Cook and drain the pasta and return it to the warm pan. Add the mushrooms, asparagus and artichokes to the pasta and cook over low heat stirring frequently for 2–3 minutes, until piping hot.

Remove the pan from the heat, add the pesto and ham and toss well. Serve immediately in warm bowls, sprinkled with shredded basil leaves and Parmesan shavings.

calabrese and broccoli arabesque

65 g/½ cup pine nuts, reserving a few to serve

50 g/½ cup sultanas/golden raisins

500 g/4 heaped cups fresh broccoli florets

1½ tablespoons tomato purée/paste

100 ml/⅓ cup warm water

100 ml/⅓ cup olive oil

1 onion, finely sliced

1 x 50-g/2-oz can anchovies, drained thoroughly and patted dry with paper towels

50 ml/¼ cup scalding hot milk

To serve

freshly cooked pasta of your choice (see page 140)

torn fresh coriander/cilantro leaves

freshly grated pecorino or Parmesan

Serves 4

This unusual vegetable sauce, enhanced with sultanas, anchovies and pine nuts, explodes with flavour. It is based on a classic recipe popular in parts of southern Italy and Sicily, where ingredients such as sultanas and pine nuts show an Arab influence – arabesque.

Put the pine nuts in a dry frying pan/skillet and heat gently until golden brown all over. Take care, because they burn easily. Remove to a plate and let cool.

Soak the sultanas/golden raisins in boiling water for 15 minutes, then drain and pat dry with paper towels. Cook the broccoli in a large saucepan of boiling salted water until just soft, 5–10 minutes. Drain well.

Put the tomato purée/paste in a small bowl, add the warm water and stir to dilute. Heat half the olive oil in a sauté pan, then add the onion and tomato purée/paste mixture. Cook over low heat until softened, then add the boiled broccoli.

Use a fork to mash the anchovies in a small bowl, then stir in the hot milk and remaining olive oil to form a smooth paste. Pour over the vegetables, add the sultanas/golden raisins and pine nuts (reserving some to serve), stir well and cover with a lid. Turn off the heat and set aside to develop the flavours.

Add the sauce to the pasta, stir well, then transfer to a large serving dish. Add the coriander and reserved pine nuts. Serve at once with grated pecorino or Parmesan.

aubergine and tomato sauce

Aubergines make a substantial and filling sauce and carry the flavours of garlic and good olive oil well.

2 aubergines/eggplant, cut into bite-size cubes

500 g/1 lb 2 oz ripe tomatoes, quartered and deseeded

2 garlic cloves, halved

4 tablespoons olive oil

1 shallot, finely chopped

2 tablespoons chopped fresh mint

2 tablespoons chopped fresh coriander/cilantro

freshly squeezed juice of 1 lemon

salt and freshly ground black pepper

freshly cooked pasta of your choice to serve (see page 140)

Serves 4

Preheat the oven 200°C (400°F) Gas 6.

Put the aubergine/eggplant, tomatoes and garlic in a large roasting pan. Add 2 tablespoons of the olive oil and mix. Season with salt and pepper and cook in the preheated oven for 30–40 minutes, turning from time to time, until the aubergine/eggplant is tender and golden. Meanwhile cook the pasta.

Drain the pasta and add the roasted aubergine/eggplant and tomatoes, then the shallot, mint, coriander/cilantro and lemon juice. Pour in the remaining oil and toss well to mix before serving.

This is a lovely and unusual pasta sauce, well-suited to the season when walnuts and all kinds of orange-fleshed squashes will be at their best. In Northern Italy, a version of this walnut sauce is traditionally served with pappardelle pasta, but it is good with other shapes too, including, strange though it may seem (and distinctly unItalian), wholemeal spaghetti.

pan-fried squash, walnut and parsley sauce

150 g/1 heaped cup walnut halves

2–3 garlic cloves, peeled

5 tablespoons olive oil

1 tablespoon walnut oil

5 tablespoons double/heavy cream or crème fraîche

leaves from a small bunch of fresh flat-leaf parsley

freshly squeezed lemon juice, to taste

650 g/4–5 cups prepared, cubed squash (1-cm/¼-inch square)

1–2 pinches dried chilli/hot red pepper flakes, crushed

freshly grated nutmeg, to taste

sea salt and freshly ground black pepper

To serve

freshly cooked pasta of your choice (see page 140), reserving 4–5 tablespoons of cooking water

freshly grated Parmesan

Serves 4

Preheat the oven to 180°C (350°F) Gas 4.

Put the walnuts on a baking sheet and toast them in the preheated oven for 5–6 minutes, making sure they don't burn. Turn them onto a dry, clean linen cloth and rub vigorously to remove as much of the skin as possible. Chop a third of the nuts roughly and set aside then put the remaining ones in a food processor. Blanch the garlic in boiling water for 2–3 minutes, drain and rinse. Put the garlic in the processor with the walnuts, add 2 tablespoons of the olive oil, the walnut oil and cream. Whizz to make a paste. Set aside a third of the parsley, then whizz the remaining two-thirds into the sauce. Chop the reserved parsley and set aside. Leave the sauce in the processor until needed.

In a large frying pan/skillet, heat the remaining olive oil over medium heat, add the squash and chilli/hot pepper flakes and cook, turning the squash now and then, until it is tender and lightly browned, about 10–12 minutes. Meanwhile, bring a large saucepan of salted water to the boil and cook the pasta according to the packet instructions.

Whizz enough of the reserved pasta-cooking water into the sauce to make it creamy, then season with salt, pepper and a little nutmeg. Toss the pasta with the squash, remaining walnuts and parsley and a little of the sauce. Serve the Parmesan and remaining sauce at the table.

mushroom and marsala sauce

50 g/3½ tablespoons unsalted butter

1 garlic clove, crushed

a handful of fresh flat-leaf parsley, chopped

250 g/4 cups thinly sliced button mushrooms

2½ tablespoons Marsala wine or sweet sherry

125 ml/½ cup vegetable stock

250 ml/1 cup single/light cream

3 tablespoons freshly grated Parmesan

sea salt and freshly ground black pepper

To serve

freshly cooked pasta of your choice (see page 140)

chopped fresh flat-leaf parsley

freshly grated Parmesan

Serves 4

This is a rich, aromatic cream pasta sauce flavoured with mushrooms, very slowly cooked in garlic, parsley and Marsala. Keep a bottle of Marsala in the cupboard for cooking – it has a very distinctive flavour and is useful for both sweet and savoury dishes. It is used frequently in Bolognese cooking, and in Sicily where it is made. This sauce also goes well with pan-fried steak, veal and pork.

To make the mushroom sauce, melt the butter in a frying pan/skillet. Add the garlic, parsley and mushrooms and cook gently over low heat, stirring from time to time. When the mushrooms have reduced and starting to soften, add the Marsala and salt and pepper to taste. Stir well, cover the pan with a lid and let cook for a further 30 minutes, adding a little stock from time to time. The mushrooms should be moist, but not watery. Add the cream and heat gently, shaking the pan from time to time.

Add the sauce and the Parmesan to the freshly cooked pasta. Sprinkle with chopped parsley and serve at once with extra Parmesan.

courgette, mint, lemon and cream sauce

This makes a deliciously summery pasta that's full of flavour. You can make it with either green or yellow courgettes (the smaller the better), or you could use little Pattypan summer squashes. You could also toss some shredded golden yellow courgette flowers in at the very last moment to barely wilt in the heat of the pasta.

40 g/2½ tablespoons butter

300–350 g/2 cups thinly sliced baby courgettes/zucchini

125 ml/½ cup dry vermouth, such as Noilly Prat (optional)

150 ml/⅔ cup double/heavy cream or crème fraîche

finely grated zest of 1 large unwaxed lemon

freshly squeezed lemon juice, to taste

2 tablespoons fresh mint leaves, chopped if on the large side

sea salt and freshly ground black pepper

To serve

freshly cooked pasta of your choice (see page 140), reserving 5–7 tablespoons of cooking water

3–4 tablespoons toasted pine nuts

a few courgette flowers/squash blossoms (optional)

Serves 2

Melt the butter in a frying pan/skillet set over low heat and add the courgettes/zucchini and a pinch of salt. Cook gently for about 10 minutes until tender but barely browned.

Turn up the heat under the courgettes/zucchini and add the vermouth (if using) or 4–5 tablespoons of the cooking water and let it bubble and evaporate. Add the cream and lemon zest, and again let it bubble, reduce and thicken slightly. If it reduces too much, add another 1–2 tablespoons cooking water. Sharpen with a squeeze or 2 of lemon juice as necessary and toss with the pasta and mint.

Serve immediately with a grinding of black pepper and a sprinkling of toasted pine nuts.

Fish and seafood can be used to create delicious pasta sauces. Fresh or smoked oily fish works well with cream, as do scallops; white fish suits butter or olive oil while shellfish goes with olive oil, chilli and parsley or with tomato.

fish and seafood

rich seafood sauce

This is the perfect sauce for a lavish occasion. The rich tomato concassé infused with saffron provides a perfect base for fresh seafood, to serve with spaghetti or linguine.

3 tablespoons extra virgin olive oil, plus extra to drizzle

2 garlic cloves, chopped

1 tablespoon chopped fresh thyme

650 g/1½ lbs ripe tomatoes, skinned and finely chopped

150 ml/⅔ cup dry white wine

150 ml/⅔ cup fish stock

a small pinch of saffron threads

2 x 350-g/12-oz uncooked lobster tails

12 fresh mussels

12 large scallops

12 large uncooked prawns/shrimp, shelled and deveined

2 tablespoons chopped fresh basil

sea salt and freshly ground black pepper

freshly cooked pasta of your choice (see page 140) to serve

Serves 4

Heat the olive oil in a large, wide saucepan and gently fry the garlic and thyme for 3–4 minutes, or until soft but not browned. Add the tomatoes, stir well, then pour in the wine. Bring to the boil and simmer for 1 minute, then add the stock, saffron and seasoning. Cover and simmer over low heat for 30 minutes.

Meanwhile, prepare the shellfish. Cut the lobster tails lengthways down the centre of the back and discard any intestinal tract, then cut, through the shell, into 4–5 pieces. (You can leave the shell on or take it off before cooking – if you leave it on, be sure to warn guests to watch out for the shell in the sauce.) Wash the mussels in several changes of cold water, scrub the shells clean and pull out the straggly 'beard' if still attached. Cut away the tough grey muscle at the side of each scallop.

Add the lobster and mussels to the tomato sauce and cook for 5 minutes, or until the mussels have opened. Discard any that remain closed. Add the prawns/shrimp and cook for a further 2 minutes, then add the scallops and cook for a further minute. Remove the pan from the heat and stir in the basil. Serve hot, drizzled with extra oil.

180 ml/¾ cup extra virgin olive oil

450 g/1 lb lobster meat, from
a 1-kg/2-lb-4-oz whole lobster,
or prawn/shrimp or crab meat

1 small bunch of fresh dill,
chopped

1 bunch of fresh chives, chopped

shredded zest and juice
of 1 unwaxed lemon

sea salt and freshly ground
black pepper

freshly cooked pasta of your
choice (see page 140) to serve

Serves 4

lobster sauce

**Olive oil is the perfect vehicle for pasta sauces and marries well
with elegant ingredients such as lobster, prawns/shrimp or crab.
It makes this pasta a special-occasion dish, especially when
served with homemade tagliatelle (see pages 132–137).**

Warm the oil in a heavy-based frying pan/skillet. Add the lobster,
prawn/shrimp or crab meat, dill, chives, 1 tablespoon of the lemon
juice and salt and pepper. Heat briefly until the flavours blend well.
Leave on a very low heat to keep warm.

Tip the cooked pasta into the sauce, toss gently with 2 wooden
spoons, add the lemon zest and serve immediately.

smoked salmon,
creme fraiche and dill sauce

150 g/¾–1 cup julienne strips of smoked salmon (or trimmings)

4 tablespoons crème fraîche or double/heavy cream

freshly ground black pepper, to taste

a small bunch of fresh dill or chives, as preferred

freshly cooked pasta of your choice (see page 140) to serve, reserving 3–4 tablespoons of cooking water

Serves 4

Strips of smoked salmon turn the creamy sauce for this pasta an attractive pink. Freshly snipped fresh chives or dill add a strong flavour and make this a satisfyingly quick and easy dish, as well as a delicious one!

Put the salmon strips in a small saucepan. Add the cream and about 3 grinds of black pepper.

Set the pan over the lowest possible heat and warm until cream melts and the salmon turns a pale pink. Turn off the heat. Stir in as much of the reserved pasta cooking water as necessary to make a pourable sauce.

Tip the cooked pasta into a large serving bowl and pour the sauce over the top. Toss the pasta until well mixed. Using kitchen scissors, snip the chives or dill straight onto the pasta.

Variation
Add 125 g/1 cup frozen peas or canned sweetcorn kernels to the sauce before you add the pepper.

monkfish and italian vegetables with olives and capers

500 g/1 lb 2 oz monkfish tail

4 tablespoons olive oil

2 shallots, finely chopped

4 baby courgettes/zucchini sliced into bite-size pieces

1 large red (bell) pepper, halved, deseeded and cut into bite-size pieces

125 ml/½ cup white wine

2½ tablespoons capers, rinsed if salted

6 medium tomatoes, skinned, deseeded and chopped

1½ tablespoons pitted black olives

sea salt and freshly ground black pepper

To serve

freshly cooked pasta of your choice (see page 140)

a handful of fresh basil or flat-leaf parsley leaves, finely chopped

extra virgin olive oil

Serves 4–6

One of the highlights of a holiday in Italy is an early morning visit to a fish market. Whole tuna and swordfish, boxes of squid and prawns/shrimp of every size and variety, ray and turbot, scabbard fish coiled into boxes like ties in a drawer, small sharks with eerie grey skin and the extraordinary monkfish, cowled in more fleshy folds than a bloodhound. This is fresh!

Preheat the oven to 200°C (400°F) Gas 6.

Wipe the fish and cut into 4 equal pieces, discarding any bones. Season well with salt and pepper, arrange in an oiled roasting pan and set aside.

Heat the oil in a frying pan/skillet, then add the shallots. Cook until soft, then raise the heat, add the courgettes/zucchini and (bell) peppers and brown quickly. Add the wine, and when it has evaporated, add the capers, stir well, then add salt and pepper to taste.

Spoon the cooked vegetables over the fish in the roasting pan until covered. Add the chopped tomatoes, olives and extra olive oil. Cover the pan with foil and cook in the preheated oven for 8 minutes. Remove from the oven, discard the foil, cut the fish into bite-size pieces and mix carefully into the vegetables.

Add the fish and vegetables and their cooking juices to the cooked pasta and mix well, then stir in the basil or parsley and oil.

Variations
Try thick cod, halibut, salmon or haddock fillets rather than monkfish tails.

300 g/2 cups cherry tomatoes

1 tablespoon extra virgin olive oil plus extra for cooking

2 onions, finely sliced

1 teaspoon crushed coriander seeds

2 x 160-g/6-oz cans of tuna in oil, lightly drained

1½ tablespoons capers, rinsed if salted

finely grated zest of 1 unwaxed lemon

125 ml/½ cup milk

sea salt and freshly ground black pepper

To serve

freshly cooked pasta of your choice (see page 140)

a handful of fresh mint leaves

Serves 4–6

This is a delicious lunch or light dinner dish made with ingredients that, although not all strictly from the store-cupboard, are to be found in most kitchens.

tuna, coriander seed and lemon zest

Cut a cross in the top and bottom of the tomatoes, then plunge them briefly into boiling water. Drain, pull off the skins, then remove the seeds and cores. Cut the flesh into small cubes. Add the oil, mint, salt and pepper to taste and set aside to develop the flavours.

Cover the base of a frying pan/skillet with olive oil, add the onions and coriander seeds and cook slowly over medium heat. When the onions start to soften, add 3 tablespoons water and cover with a lid. Continue cooking over low heat until soft. This will take 15 minutes – do not rush (add extra water if necessary).

When the onions are very soft, add the tuna, capers, lemon zest, lots of black pepper and half the milk. Stir well, cover again and cook for 10 minutes over low heat (add the remaining milk if necessary).

Add the sauce and the diced tomatoes to the freshly cooked pasta and mix well. Sprinkle with mint leaves and serve at once.

chilli tuna tartare

6 tablespoons extra virgin olive oil

4 garlic cloves, sliced

1–2 dried red chillies, deseeded and chopped

grated zest and juice of 1 unwaxed lemon

1 tablespoon fresh thyme leaves

a 500-g/1-lb sashimi-grade fresh tuna steak chopped into very small cubes

a handful of fresh basil leaves

sea salt and freshly ground black pepper

freshly cooked pasta of your choice (see page 140), to serve, reserving 3–4 tablespoons of cooking water

Serves 4

'Tartare' means uncooked and, to serve fish this way, you must use very fresh, sashimi-grade tuna. If you prefer your tuna cooked, sear it on a preheated stove-top grill pan for 1 minute on each side or until cooked to your liking.

Cook the pasta according to the instructions on the packet.

Meanwhile, heat the oil in a frying pan/skillet, add the garlic and fry gently for 2 minutes until lightly golden. Add the chilli, lemon zest and thyme and fry for a further 1 minute.

Drain the pasta, reserving 3–4 tablespoons on the cooking water and return both to the pan. Stir in the hot garlic oil mixture, the lemon juice, the raw tuna, basil leaves, salt and pepper and a little extra olive oil. Serve immediately.

If you have friends coming round for a mid-week meal and you need to make something special but don't want to spend more than 10 minutes in the kitchen, this simple yet impressive recipe provides the answer.

chilli scallops

Rinse the scallops in cold water and discard the black vein, if necessary. Pat dry on paper towels. If the scallops are large, cut them into 2 or 3 slices.

Cook the pasta and return it to the pan with the reserved cooking water to keep warm.

Put the garlic, chillies and coriander/cilantro in a small bowl and mix. Heat a heavy-based frying pan/skillet and add 1 tablespoon of the oil. Add the chilli mixture to the pan and cook for 1 minute, stirring, then add the scallops. Stir well until coated with the oil and chillies. Cook, stirring occasionally, for 2–3 minutes, until the scallops are cooked. Season to taste with salt and pepper. Keep them warm in a low oven.

Add the cream and remaining oil to the spaghetti and reheat gently, stirring frequently, until piping hot. Serve immediately, topped with the scallops.

Variation

Any seafood or shellfish, such as baby squid, would work well with this recipe. To prepare squid, rinse in cold water, discard the quill, remove the tentacles and trim. Slice the squid if large, but leave whole if small. Cook as above for 2–3 minutes, or until cooked. Serve as for the main recipe.

16–24 fresh scallops

4 garlic cloves, coarsely chopped

1–2 fresh red chillies, deseeded and coarsely chopped

1 tablespoon chopped fresh coriander/cilantro

2 tablespoons extra virgin olive oil

125 ml/½ cup single/light cream

sea salt and freshly ground black pepper

freshly cooked pasta of your choice (see page 140) to serve, reserving 2 tablespoons of the cooking water

Serves 4

grilled prawns and salmon with basil and citrus cream sauce

100 g/4 oz peeled cooked prawns/shrimp

150 g/5 oz small uncooked prawns/shrimp with shells on

200 ml/¾ cup single/light cream

50 g/3½ tablespoons unsalted butter

a 200-g/7-oz thick salmon fillet, sliced thinly across the grain of the fish

finely grated zest of 1 unwaxed lemon and freshly squeezed juice of ½

extra virgin olive oil, to taste

about 20 fresh basil leaves, shredded

sea salt and freshly ground black pepper

freshly cooked pasta of your choice (see page 140) to serve

a stove-top grill pan

Serves 4

Here is a deliciously indulgent recipe, perfect for summer entertaining. If preferred you can substitute hot smoked salmon fillets for the salmon fillet and simply flake them into the finished dish before serving.

Put the peeled prawns/shrimp in a food processor and blend to a paste. Put the cream, butter and freshly ground black pepper in a small saucepan and heat gently, shaking the pan from time to time. When the sauce has thickened, add the prawn/shrimp paste to the cream, stir, cover and switch off the heat.

Preheat a stove-top grill pan until very hot. Arrange the strips of salmon fillet across the ridges of the pan and cook quickly on both sides. Transfer the pieces to a plate as they brown, sprinkle with oil, lemon juice, salt and pepper.

Pan-grill the unshelled prawns, in batches if necessary, until aromatic, opaque and pink. Set aside 8–12 prawns/shrimp and 4 slices of the salmon for serving.

Add the sauce, prawns/shrimp, salmon pieces and basil to the freshly cooked pasta and mix well. Divide between 4 pasta bowls. Make small piles of the reserved prawns/shrimp and salmon on the top of each portion and sprinkle with lemon zest. Serve immediately.

baby clams with tarragon and cherry tomatoes

There's something pure about linguine alle vongole, which is redolent of the seaside and its salty air. The cherry tomatoes and tarragon freshen up the whole thing. If you can't get fresh clams, used canned ones or mussels instead.

750 g/1 lb 10 oz clams, cleaned and scrubbed

150 ml/⅔ cup dry white wine or vermouth

6 tablespoons extra virgin olive oil

2 garlic cloves, peeled and thinly sliced

¼ teaspoon dried chilli/hot red pepper flakes

250 g/1 cup small cherry tomatoes, halved

leaves from 3 fresh tarragon sprigs, finely chopped

freshly ground black pepper

freshly cooked pasta of your choice though linguine is recommended (see page 140) to serve

Serves 4

First discard any clams that do not shut when tapped sharply against the worktop.

Pour the white wine into a large saucepan and bring to the boil over high heat, then add the clams. Cover tightly with a lid, wait a couple of minutes, then stir so the unopened clams fall to the bottom. Replace the lid and cook for a further 2 minutes. By this time all the clams should be open; discard any that remain closed. Transfer the remainder to a bowl with all the cooking liquid and set aside until needed.

Add 3 tablespoons of the olive oil to the clam pan, then add the garlic, chilli flakes and cherry tomatoes. Cook over medium heat for a few minutes until the tomatoes burst and soften. Spoon in the cooked clams and strain in about 200 ml/¾ cup of the reserved cooking liquid. Cook over high heat until the liquid boils.

Toss the cooked pasta with the clams, tarragon, remaining olive oil and lots of freshly ground black pepper. Serve immediately.

The joy of meat and poultry sauces is that they often improve when made in advance, so they can simply be reheated in the time it takes to cook the pasta. They keep well and freeze well, so always make a double quantity.

meat and poultry

olive oil, for cooking

200 g/7 oz pancetta cubes or 5 slices streaky bacon, cut into small pieces

a piece of dried chilli, to taste

1 onion, finely chopped

2 x 400-g/14-oz cans whole plum tomatoes, drained (retain the juice), deseeded and chopped

3 tablespoons freshly grated pecorino or Parmesan

sea salt and freshly ground black pepper

To serve

freshly cooked pasta of your choice (see page 140)

a handful of fresh flat-leaf parsley leaves, chopped

extra virgin olive oil, to drizzle

freshly grated Parmesan

Serves 4–6

This recipe comes originally from Le Marche (pronounced 'lay mar-kay') region of Italy, but it is also synonymous with the robust traditional cooking of Rome. The sauce is made with fried pancetta and onions, flavoured with chilli and cooked in tomato. Traditionally it is served with bucatini, thick spaghetti-like pasta with a hole running though the middle.

spicy bacon and tomato sauce

Cover the base of a frying pan/skillet with olive oil, then set over medium heat until a haze starts to rise. Add the pancetta or bacon and the chilli. Cook until the fat runs, then add the onion. Fry over low heat until the onion is transparent.

Add the tomatoes, cover with a lid and cook over low heat for 30 minutes. Stir often to prevent sticking, adding a little of the tomato juice to the pan if necessary. Discard the chilli. Add salt and pepper to taste. At this stage the sauce can be rested and reheated when required.

When ready to serve, cook the pasta, then stir in the sauce, 3 tablespoons cheese and the parsley. Drizzle with extra oil and serve at once with extra Parmesan.

broad beans and bacon

Broad beans/fava taste delicious mixed with a lightly smoked bacon and grated cheese. This is one of the easiest pasta sauces you can make – try it with fresh or frozen peas if broad beans/fava are not in season.

1 garlic clove, peeled

200 g/7 oz good-quality chopped bacon, lardons or pancetta cubes

170 ml/¾ cup double/heavy cream

about 350 g/3½ cups shelled broad beans/fava

a small handful of fresh basil or mint leaves, snipped with scissors

pasta of your choice (see page 140) to serve (it can be cooked along with the broad beans/fava)

freshly ground black pepper

grated Parmesan, to serve

Serves 4

Using a rolling pin slightly squash the garlic clove. This will help to release the garlicky flavour into the sauce.

Set a heavy-based saucepan or deep frying pan on the hob over high heat. Add the bacon and fry for 1 minute. Turn the heat down, add the garlic clove and fry, stirring occasionally, until the bacon is cooked and just beginning to go slightly crisp. Add the cream and stir. Turn off the heat and leave to one side.

Put the pasta on to cook and add the broad beans/fava into the water about 4 minutes before the pasta is ready. Drain the beans and the pasta and return to the saucepan.

Taste the sauce, remove the garlic clove and add the fresh herbs. Season with freshly ground black pepper. Add the sauce to the pan with the cooked pasta and broad beans and heat gently over low heat until warmed through. Serve immediately with plenty of freshly grated black pepper and grated Parmesan.

The difference between this carbonara and the more traditional recipe on page 34 is that here skimmed milk is used instead of the usual egg yolks and cream. However, the white wine, extra-lean bacon and fresh herbs ensure there is no compromise on taste!

light and creamy carbonara sauce

8 slices extra-lean bacon, fat removed and thinly sliced

140 g/2 cups sliced button mushrooms

1 tablespoon olive oil

1 teaspoon wholegrain mustard

2 tablespoons white wine or vegetable stock

30 g/2 oz extra-mature/sharp Cheddar cheese, grated

3 teaspoons cornflour/cornstarch

250 ml/1 cup skimmed/fat-free milk

2 tablespoons chopped fresh flat-leaf parsley

To serve

freshly cooked pasta of your choice (see page 140)

freshly ground black pepper

freshly grated or shaved Parmesan

Serves 4

Heat a non-stick frying pan/skillet, add the bacon and cook over high heat for 5 minutes, until browned, turning once. Add the sliced mushrooms and oil to the pan and cook for 2 minutes. Stir in the mustard and wine or stock and cook for a further 3 minutes. Reduce the heat, add the grated Cheddar and stir until melted. Blend the cornflour/cornstarch with 2 tablespoons of water. Add to the pan and stir over low heat until the mixture becomes quite thick.

Remove the pan from the heat and let cool slightly. Season to taste with pepper, then gradually add the milk, stirring continuously until well combined. Do not heat the sauce at this stage or it may curdle. Stir in the parsley.

Drain the pasta and return it to the warm pan. Pour the carbonara sauce over the spaghetti and toss gently to mix. Serve immediately, sprinkled with Parmesan.

Variation

Try using one grilled, sliced chicken breast instead of the bacon.
For a vegetarian alternative, substitute some broccoli florets or frozen peas for the bacon.

300 g/10 oz chicken thighs, boneless and skinless

50 g/2 oz pancetta cubes or 2 slices streaky bacon

a handful of fresh flat-leaf parsley

3 tablespoons olive oil

3 tablespoons white wine

1 garlic clove, finely chopped

1 teaspoon chopped fresh marjoram leaves or a pinch of dried marjoram

400-g/14-oz can whole plum tomatoes, drained, deseeded and chopped

sea salt and freshly ground black pepper

Garlic breadcrumbs

4 tablespoons olive oil

25 g/½ cup fresh breadcrumbs

1 teaspoon finely chopped fresh marjoram

1 garlic clove, finely chopped

To serve

freshly cooked pasta of your choice (see page 140)

freshly grated Parmesan (optional)

Serves 4–6

herbed chicken with garlic breadcrumbs

Garlic breadcrumbs are served with pasta all over the meridione (southern Italy) instead of cheese, particularly with old-fashioned traditional dishes such as vermicelli alla carrettiere. This goes back to the days when every region had to rely totally on its own produce. The south was very poor indeed and there was no dairy farming to speak of, so consequently little or no cheese, but every household would have some stale bread.

To make the herbed chicken, cut each chicken thigh into 6–10 bite-size pieces. Put the pancetta and parsley together and chop finely. Heat the oil in a heavy-based saucepan, add the chopped mixture and fry over low heat until transparent. Add the chicken pieces and fry until brown. Add the white wine and heat until evaporated. Add the garlic, marjoram, tomatoes and salt and pepper to taste. Cover with a lid and cook gently for 30 minutes. Stir from time to time. At this stage the sauce can be rested and reheated when required.

To make the garlic breadcrumbs, heat the olive oil in a frying pan/skillet. Put the breadcrumbs, chopped marjoram and garlic in a bowl and mix well. When the oil starts to haze, add the breadcrumb mixture and fry until crisp and golden. Transfer to a plate covered with paper towels and let drain and cool.

Add the sauce to the cooked pasta and mix well. Sprinkle with garlic breadcrumbs and serve immediately with Parmesan, if using.

breaded garlicky chicken with parsley

3 skinless chicken breasts

1 egg, beaten

75 g/1 generous cup fresh white breadcrumbs

4 tablespoons plain/all-purpose flour

3–4 tablespoons olive oil

75 g/5 tablespoons butter

2 garlic cloves, crushed

a small handful of fresh flat-leaf parsley leaves, chopped

sea salt and freshly ground black pepper

To serve

Parmesan shavings (optional)

freshly cooked pasta of your choice (see page 140), reserving 250 ml/1 cup of cooking water

Serves 4

Here the much-loved flavour and crunch of chicken Kiev is served with pasta. This isn't a traditional Italian recipe, but the thick strands of pasta soak up the buttery juices and make this perfect comfort food. Turkey escalopes or cod fillets work just as well.

Prepare one bowl with the beaten egg and another with the breadcrumbs. Put one chicken breast in a freezer bag and hit it with a rolling pin until flattened out. Spoon some of the flour into the bag, season well and shake until the chicken is coated. Dip the chicken in the egg, then in the breadcrumbs and set aside. Repeat the entire process with the remaining chicken breasts.

Heat the oil in a large frying pan/skillet over medium heat and add the chicken in a single layer. Cook for 2–3 minutes, then turn over and cook the other side for the same amount of time, or until both sides are golden. Lift the chicken onto a chopping board. Add the butter to the pan along with the garlic and parsley and leave to cook over low heat until the garlic and butter are about to colour. Season generously. Cut the chicken into strips and return to the pan.

Cook and drain the pasta (reserving about 250 ml/1 cup of the water), slide it all back into the pan you cooked it in and tip in the chicken with all its juices. Give it a good stir, add the reserved water to keep the pasta moist and transfer to bowls. Scatter over Parmesan shavings (if using) and serve immediately.

Tomato sauce

olive oil, for cooking

1 small onion, finely chopped

1 small carrot, finely chopped

½ celery stalk, finely chopped

2 x 400-g/14-oz cans whole plum tomatoes, drained (retain the juices), deseeded and chopped

about 20 fresh basil leaves

sea salt and freshly ground black pepper

Meatballs

125 g/5 oz (⅔ cup) lean minced/ground pork

50 g/¼ cup freshly grated pecorino

75 g/about 2 small soft dinner (bread) rolls, soaked in milk and squeezed dry

a handful of fresh flat-leaf parsley leaves, chopped

1 small garlic clove, chopped

1 egg

1 tablespoon red wine

plain/all-purpose flour, for rolling

vegetable oil, for frying

To serve

freshly cooked pasta of your choice (see page 140)

about 50 g/¼ cup freshly grated pecorino

a handful of fresh basil leaves

Serves 4–6

pork mini meatballs

Meatballs in tomato sauce are synonymous with early immigrants to the US from southern Italy – and no wonder, because it still plays an important part in the food of this region.

To make the tomato sauce, cover the base of a frying pan/skillet with olive oil and heat gently. Add the onion, carrot and celery and cook over low heat until soft. Do not let brown. Add the tomatoes and basil, season with salt and pepper, cover with a lid and cook for 30 minutes. Stir from time to time, adding a little reserved tomato juice if necessary.

To make the meatballs, put the meat, pecorino, bread, parsley, garlic, eggs and red wine in a bowl and season. Mix well and refrigerate for 1 hour. Take small teaspoons of the mixture and roll into tiny balls, flouring your hands as you work.

The meatballs may be deep-fried or shallow-fried in batches in vegetable oil. If using a deep-fryer, follow the manufacturer's instructions.

As each meatball is done, remove with a slotted spoon and drain on paper towels. When all the meatballs have been fried and drained, put them into the tomato sauce and cook over gentle heat for 10 minutes. At this point, the sauce can be set aside and reheated when required.

When ready to serve, add the reheated sauce to the freshly cooked pasta, add the pecorino and mix well. Top with basil leaves and serve immediately with extra pecorino.

Tomato sauce

4 tablespoons olive oil

3 garlic cloves, thinly sliced

1 large onion, cut into wedges

2 x 400-g/14-oz cans chopped tomatoes

a large handful of fresh basil leaves, shredded

sea salt and freshly ground black pepper

Meatballs

250 g/1 generous cup minced/ground beef

100 g/1½ cups fresh white breadcrumbs

2 eggs, lightly beaten

25 g/1 oz freshly grated Parmesan cheese (plus extra to serve)

4 tablespoons chopped fresh flat-leaf parsley

3 tablespoons olive oil

To serve

freshly cooked pasta of your choice to serve (see page 140)

freshly chopped basil

finely grated Parmesan

Serves 4

Don't be put off by amount of breadcrumbs used here – it not only makes this a thrifty recipe but the bread lightens the meatballs and they absorb much more of the sauce and flavoursome oil released by the meat. Accompany with a Chianti.

beef polpetti in tomato sauce

To make the tomato sauce, put the olive oil, garlic, onion, tomatoes and basil in a saucepan, season well and bring to the boil. Reduce the heat and simmer gently for at least 40 minutes while you prepare the meatballs.

Preheat the oven to 200°C (400°F) Gas 6. To make the meatballs, put the minced/ground beef, breadcrumbs, eggs, Parmesan, parsley and olive oil in a large mixing bowl, season and combine with your hands. Shape the mixture into roughly 20 walnut-size balls and put in a single layer on a baking sheet covered with foil. Roast for 10 minutes, turn, then roast for a further 6–7 minutes.

Put a saucepan of salted water on to boil for the pasta. Cook and drain the pasta, return it to the pan and add the tomato sauce and meatballs. Stir very gently so as not to break up the meatballs. Take out the onion wedges if you prefer. Scatter over a little chopped basil and grated Parmesan. Serve immediately.

ligurian meat sauce with tomato, mushrooms and pine nuts

10 g/½ scant cup dried porcini mushrooms

milk as required (see method)

3 tablespoons olive oil

1 onion, finely chopped

100 g/generous ½ cup lean minced/ground beef

25 g/¼ cup pine nuts

400-g/14-oz can whole plum tomatoes, drained (reserve the juices), deseeded and chopped

1 tablespoon finely chopped mixed fresh rosemary needles and thyme leaves

3 tablespoons freshly grated Parmesan

sea salt and freshly ground black pepper

To serve

freshly cooked pasta of your choice (see page 140)

2 teaspoons freshly chopped mixed rosemary needles and thyme leaves

freshly grated Parmesan

Serves 4–6

This meat sauce is from Liguria and differs from the rich ragù from Bologna on page 25. It is a light sauce, typical of the cooking of this region. A small amount of meat is swelled with tomatoes, mushrooms and pine nuts. Traditionally, it would be served with homemade trenette or ravioli.

Put the mushrooms in a bowl, add enough milk to cover, then soak for 15 minutes. Squeeze them dry and chop finely. Discard the milk.

Heat the olive oil in a large saucepan, add the onion and cook over low heat until soft. Increase the heat, add the meat and fry until browned. Add the pine nuts, mushrooms, tomatoes and herbs and season with salt and pepper. Stir well and cover with a lid. Reduce the heat and cook slowly for 1 hour. Stir at regular intervals and, if necessary, add a little of the reserved tomato juice to keep the sauce moist.

Add the sauce and Parmesan to the freshly cooked pasta and mix well. Serve at once sprinkled with the extra herbs. Serve extra cheese.

Variation
Use minced pork, veal or lean lamb instead of beef.

2 tablespoons olive oil

400 g/2 cups minced/ground pork

1 onion, finely chopped

2 garlic cloves, thinly sliced

4 anchovy fillets in oil, drained

2 tablespoons fresh rosemary needles

finely grated zest and juice of 1 unwaxed lemon

500 ml/2 cups milk

75 g/½ cup pitted green olives, chopped

75 ml/⅓ cup double/heavy cream

a good grating of fresh nutmeg

sea salt and freshly ground black pepper

To serve

freshly cooked pasta of your choice though rigatoni is recommended (see page 140)

4 tablespoons Parmesan shavings, plus extra to garnish

Serves 4

pork and lemon ragù sauce

In Italy, pork is often braised with milk, as it tenderizes the meat and the juices mingle with the milk to provide a sweet, meaty sauce. Rosemary is lovely and robust with pork but you could use chopped sage if you prefer – just add it earlier when you brown the pork so it frazzles a little.

Heat the olive oil in a large frying pan/skillet set over high heat and add the pork. Leave it for a few minutes until it browns, then turn it over and allow the other side to brown too. Add the onion, garlic, anchovies, rosemary and lemon zest and stir to combine with the pork. Reduce the heat, cover and leave the onion to soften for 10 minutes, stirring occasionally so the ingredients don't stick to the bottom of the pan.

When the onion is translucent, add the milk, lemon juice and olives, and bring to the boil, uncovered, scraping the base of the pan to loosen any sticky, flavoursome bits and incorporating them into the sauce. Simmer for about 15–20 minutes, or until about two-thirds of the liquid has evaporated and the pork is soft. Stir in the cream, then season with salt, pepper and nutmeg to taste.

Cook and drain the pasta, put it back into its pan and spoon in the sauce. Add the Parmesan shavings, stir well and serve immediately. Sprinkle the extra Parmesan shavings on top.

country sausage, pea and tomato sauce

This version of a traditional country recipe uses Italian sausages rather than pancetta as its base. The contrast in flavour and texture of the meaty coarse sausage, the sweetness of the peas and colourful cherry tomatoes works very well. Make sure you use a coarse-textured Italian-type sausage.

olive oil, for cooking

8 Italian-style sausages

200 ml/¾–1 cup chicken, beef or vegetable stock as preferred

1 small onion, finely chopped

about 1 kg/1 lb fresh peas, shelled, or 155 g/1 cup fresh or frozen peas (shelled)

1 teaspoon icing/confectioners' sugar

a handful of fresh flat-leaf parsley leaves, chopped

about 20 cherry tomatoes, halved

3 tablespoons freshly grated Parmesan, plus extra to serve

freshly cooked pasta of your choice to serve, though ridged tubetti or penne is recommended (see page 140)

Serves 4–6

Cover the base of a frying pan/skillet with olive oil, then set over medium heat. Add the sausages and cook over low heat, turning until they are brown on all sides. Pour off the excess fat and reserve. Cut the sausages in half, scrape out the meat and discard the skins. Add a little stock and deglaze the pan. Stir the resulting pan juices into the sausage meat. Simmer for a few minutes.

Pour a little of the reserved sausage fat into a clean frying pan/skillet and heat through. Add the onion and cook over gentle heat until soft. Add the peas, sugar, parsley and enough stock to cover the ingredients. Cover with a lid and cook until the peas are tender. If using frozen peas, add them with the onions and 5 tablespoons stock and heat through.

Stir the peas into the sausage meat and let simmer for about 5 minutes. When ready to serve, increase the heat, add the tomatoes and cook quickly until the edges start to wilt. Add the sauce to the freshly cooked pasta, stir in the Parmesan and mix well. Serve with extra cheese.

Variation

Instead of the peas, stir in cooked fagioli or other beans after cooking the onion. Add a few chopped tomatoes and cook for 10–15 minutes or until the tomatoes are thick and creamy. Proceed as in the main recipe.

Traditionally an Italian-style sausage is used for this rich sauce, but you could use a spicy Spanish chorizo if you prefer.

sausagemeat sauce

750 g/1 lb 10 oz fresh spicy Italian or Spanish sausage

2 tablespoons olive oil

1 onion, finely chopped

2 garlic cloves, crushed

2 tablespoons chopped fresh sage

2 x 400-g/14-oz cans chopped tomatoes

125 ml/½ cup red wine

2 tablespoons tomato purée/paste

2 tablespoons freshly chopped flat-leaf parsley

sea salt and freshly ground black pepper

freshly cooked pasta of your choice to serve (see page 140)

Serves 4–6

Split open the sausage skins, peel away and discard. Roughly chop the sausage meat, put in a food processor and pulse until coarsely ground.

Heat the olive oil in a saucepan and gently fry the onion, garlic, sage and seasoning over low heat for 10 minutes, or until soft and lightly golden. Add the sausage meat and stir-fry over medium heat for 5 minutes, or until browned.

Add the canned tomatoes, wine and tomato purée/paste, bring to the boil, cover and simmer gently for 1 hour, or until the sauce has thickened. Season to taste, stir in the parsley and serve hot with freshly cooked pasta.

aubergine, sausage and zinfandel sauce

This is a really robust pasta sauce that's perfect to serve in cold weather. The wine gives a richer, more warming flavour than the usual tomato-based sauce. Use Italian sausages with 100 per cent coarsely ground pork filling for the best result.

350 g/12 oz Italian sausages

4 tablespoons olive oil

1 aubergine/eggplant, cut into cubes

1 onion, finely chopped

1 red (bell) pepper, deseeded and cut into small cubes

1 tablespoon tomato purée/paste

2 garlic cloves, crushed

1 teaspoon dried oregano

175 ml/¾ cup Zinfandel or other full-bodied, fruity red wine

175 ml/¾ cup chicken or vegetable stock, as preferred

4 tablespoons chopped fresh flat-leaf parsley

sea salt and freshly ground black pepper

freshly cooked pasta of your choice (see page 140) to serve, reserving a few tablespoons of the cooking water

Serves 4

Slit the sausage skins with a sharp knife, peel them off and discard. Roughly chop the sausage meat. Heat 1 tablespoon of the olive oil in a large frying pan/skillet or wok, add the sausagemeat, breaking it up with a spatula or wooden spoon, and fry until lightly golden. Using a slotted spoon, remove the meat from the pan and set aside.

Add 2 more tablespoons of the oil to the pan, add the aubergine/eggplant and stir fry for 3–4 minutes until it starts to brown. Add the remaining oil and the chopped onion and fry for 1–2 minutes. Add the red (bell) pepper and fry for 1–2 minutes more. Return the sausage meat to the pan, stir in the tomato purée/paste and cook for 1 minute. Add the garlic, oregano and wine and simmer until the wine has reduced by half. Stir in the stock and let simmer over low heat for about 10 minutes.

Meanwhile cook the pasta. When the pasta is just cooked, spoon off a couple of tablespoons of the cooking water and stir it into the wine sauce. Drain the pasta thoroughly, then tip it into the sauce. Add 3 tablespoons of the parsley and mix well. Remove the pan from the heat, cover and let stand for 2–3 minutes for the flavours to amalgamate.

Check the seasoning, adding salt and pepper to taste and serve immediately, sprinkled with the remaining parsley.

Cream sauces are delicious on their own, enriched with cheese, herbs or citrus zest and stirred into egg-based or stuffed pastas. They are also useful as a base, simply add smoked fish or meat, lightly cooked vegetables or nuts.

cream, eggs and cheese

250 ml/1 cup single/light cream

1½ tablespoons unsalted butter

3 tablespoons freshly grated Parmesan

freshly ground black pepper or freshly grated nutmeg, to taste

50–100 ml/¼–⅓ cup vegetable stock (or pasta cooking water)

To serve

freshly cooked pasta of your choice though filled tortellini is recommended (see page 140)

freshly grated Parmesan cheese

3 tablespoons freshly chopped herbs, such as flat-leaf parsley, coriander/cilantro or basil

finely grated zest of ½ an unwaxed lemon

Serves 4

basic cream sauce with butter and parmesan

This basic sauce provides the departure point for a variety of other sauces. Add herbs, nuts or cheese to make a delicious sauce for stuffed pasta. Always dress the pasta in a bowl rather than the pan, because the heat of the pan will dry out dairy-based sauces.

Put the cream and butter in a shallow saucepan and set over low heat. Bring to simmering point, shaking the pan from time to time. Let simmer for a few minutes or until the sauce starts to thicken. Add the cheese and pepper or nutmeg as preferred and stir.

Stir the sauce and half of the stock (or reserved pasta cooking water) into the pasta. Mix until well coated. Add extra liquid if necessary and stir again. Serve immediately with extra Parmesan, chopped herbs and grated lemon zest, if using.

Variation

Add 100 g/5 oz finely sliced smoked salmon or trout and 3 tablespoons finely chopped dill or fennel to the pasta at the same time as the cream sauce, and stir gently.

finely grated zest of
2 unwaxed lemons

125 ml/½ cup dry vermouth

200 ml/¾ cup double/heavy
cream

50 g/⅓ cup freshly grated
Parmesan, plus extra to serve

2 tablespoons chopped fresh basil

sea salt and freshly ground
black pepper

freshly cooked pasta of your
choice (see page 140) to serve

Serves 4

lemon, cream and vermouth sauce

This is quite an unusual sauce for pasta, but no less wonderful for it. If you are unable to buy unwaxed lemons, be sure to wash the skins well before grating the zest.

Put the lemon zest and vermouth in a small saucepan, bring to the boil, then simmer until the liquid is reduced by half. Leave to cool for 5 minutes.

Beat in the cream and return to the heat until warmed through. Stir in the Parmesan and basil and season to taste. Serve at once, sprinkled with extra grated Parmesan.

The striking wine-red leaves of raddichio make a colourful and sophisticated addition to this indulgent pasta dish. The sauce is rich with saffron and a splash of Italian grappa adds depth to the flavour. Don't be tempted to add the radicchio leaves too soon as they will lose their bite and turn a disappointing dark green if cooked.

a large pinch of saffron threads or ¼ teaspoon powdered saffron

1 teaspoon sea salt flakes

2 tablespoons grappa (or other eau de vie) or hot water

3 tablespoons olive oil

2 garlic cloves, finely sliced

1 leek, white parts only, finely sliced

250 g/1 generous cup cream cheese

125 ml/½ cup white wine

To serve

50 g/2 oz Parmesan, freshly shaved into curls

cracked black pepper, to taste

12–16 baby radicchio leaves

extra virgin olive oil, to drizzle

freshly cooked pasta of your choice (see page 140) to serve

Serves 4

raddichio, saffron and cracked black pepper sauce

Put the saffron and sea salt flakes in a mortar and pound to a powder with the pestle. Add the grappa or hot water and stir to dissolve.

Heat the olive oil in a heavy-based frying pan/skillet. Add the garlic and leek and sauté for 2–3 minutes. Add the saffron liquid, cream cheese and wine. Mash and stir to form a creamy sauce. Simmer, stirring, until the wine loses its raw taste and the flavours have mellowed, about 3 minutes.

Cook and drain the pasta, toss into the sauce and stir until coated.

Serve topped with the Parmesan curls, cracked black pepper, radicchio leaves and drizzled with olive oil. Serve immediately.

1½ tablespoons unsalted butter

1 garlic clove crushed

175 g/1½ cups crumbled Gorgonzola

175 g/generous ⅔ cup mascarpone

a pinch of ground mace or a little freshly grated nutmeg

100 g/1 cup pecan halves, toasted and roughly chopped

2 tablespoons snipped fresh chives

sea salt and freshly ground black pepper

freshly cooked pasta or your choice (see page 140) to serve

Serves 4

gorgonzola, pecan and mascarpone sauce

The toasted pecan nuts add texture to this rich and creamy cheese sauce. Gorgonzola is a strongly flavoured blue cheese that is perfect combined with the milder mascarpone. Other blue cheeses you could use are Roquefort or even Stilton.

Melt the butter in a saucepan and gently fry the garlic over low heat for 2–3 minutes, or until soft but not browned. Stir in the Gorgonzola, mascarpone, mace and a little seasoning. Cook gently until the sauce is heated through but the cheese still has a little texture.

Remove the pan from the heat and stir in the pecan nuts and chives. Season to taste and serve immediately with freshly cooked pasta.

lemon, basil and parmesan cream sauce

If your brunch is a late one, this is an easy dish to whip up. You can add a splash of vodka to the shallots too, which just gives it a slight acidic edge, as wine does.

1½ tablespoons unsalted butter

2 shallots, finely chopped

1 unwaxed lemon

300 ml/1¼ cups single/light cream

200 ml/¾ cup hot vegetable stock

2 handfuls of fresh basil leaves, plus more to serve

75 g/3 oz freshly shaved Parmesan or pecorino, plus extra to serve

sea salt and freshly ground black pepper

freshly cooked pasta of your choice (see page 140) to serve

Serves 4

Heat the butter in a frying pan/skillet and add the shallots. Add a pinch of salt, cover and cook over low heat for 6–7 minutes, stirring every now and then, until soft and glossy.

Take a potato peeler and pare off the zest of the lemon, leaving behind the white pith. Try to pare the zest in one long piece so you can easily remove it later.

Add the cream, stock, lemon zest and basil to the shallots and gently simmer for 10–15 minutes, uncovered, until it has reduced and thickened – it should only just coat the back of a spoon.

Season the sauce with a little salt and lots of pepper. Fish out the lemon zest. Cook and drain the pasta and return to the pan. Stir in the Parmesan and squeeze in some juice from the lemon. Add more juice or seasoning, to taste. Garnish with more basil and Parmesan shavings and serve immediately.

Béchamel sauce

2 tablespoons unsalted butter

2 tablespoons plain/all-purpose flour

250 ml/1 cup warm milk

sea salt

freshly grated nutmeg

Vegetables

a knob/nut of unsalted butter

1 small onion, finely chopped

½ an iceberg lettuce, shredded

freshly grated nutmeg, to taste

125 g/1 cup chopped cooked ham

sea salt and freshly ground black pepper

To serve

freshly cooked pasta of your choice (see page 140)

60 g/2 oz Emmental, shaved

freshly grated Parmesan

Serves 4–6

prosciutto, emmental and lettuce sauce

Cold ham and salad never tasted as good as this simple supper dish. Finely shredded Savoy cabbage, leeks or pak choi/bok choy can be used instead of iceberg lettuce. Béchamel sauce is a very versatile base sauce to which all kinds of ingredients can be added.

To make the béchamel sauce, put the butter in a saucepan and melt until it starts to bubble. Add the flour and mix well. Cook over gentle heat for 1–2 minutes, add the milk and continue cooking until the sauce thickens. Stir constantly with a wire whisk to stop lumps forming. Add salt and grated nutmeg to taste.

To cook the vegetables, gently melt the butter in a large frying pan/skillet. Add the onion and fry over low heat until transparent. Add the lettuce and continue cooking for 5 minutes. Grate the nutmeg onto the lettuce and onion as it is cooking. When the lettuce is well wilted, add the ham and béchamel sauce and stir. Add salt and pepper to taste.

Add the sauce to the drained pasta and mix until well coated. Sprinkle with Emmental shavings and serve grated Parmesan separately.

Variation

For a vegetarian option, added 125 g/1 scant cup chopped walnuts in place of the ham.

1 garlic clove

2 large green fresh chillies, deseeded

a large handful of fresh basil leaves, plus extra to serve

2 tablespoons pine nuts

100 ml/⅓ cup extra virgin olive oil

100 g/4 oz goat cheese

250 g/1 cup fresh or frozen peas

sea salt and freshly ground black pepper

To serve

freshly cooked pasta of your choice (see page 140)

freshly grated Parmesan

Serves 4

goat cheese and basil pesto with peas

Crumbly goat cheese works surprisingly well in pesto, adding a slightly creamy edge to it. Roughly crumble it in so you get pockets of the molten cheese tucked in amongst your tangle of tagliatelle.

To make the pesto, put the garlic, chillies, basil (reserving a few leaves to serve) and a large pinch of salt in a food processor and process until roughly chopped.

Put the pine nuts in a dry frying pan/skillet and toast over low heat for a few minutes, shaking the pan, until they are golden all over. Add the pine nuts to the mixture in the food processor and process again until coarsely chopped. Add half of the olive oil and process again. Add the remaining oil, crumble in the goat cheese and stir. Taste and season.

Add the peas to a small saucepan and simmer for 4–5 minutes if frozen or 3 minutes if fresh.

Add 2–3 generous spoonfuls of pesto and the drained peas to freshly cooked pasta and toss, then add the remaining pesto making sure all the pasta is thoroughly coated.

Serve immediately garnished with the reserved basil and freshly grated Parmesan.

200 g/7 oz (1 tub) baby mozzarella balls (bocconcini), drained and halved

250 g/2 cups small cherry tomatoes, halved

4 tablespoons extra virgin olive oil

2 large handfuls of rocket/arugula

sea salt and freshly ground black pepper

To serve

freshly cooked pasta of your choice (see page 140)

extra virgin olive oil

balsamic vinegar

Serves 4–6

cherry tomatoes and mozzarella with rocket

This colourful summer dish is perfect for alfresco eating. It is more a salad than a sauce – just stir it into hot pasta and serve warm.

Put the mozzarella balls and cherry tomatoes in a large bowl. Add the olive oil, salt and freshly ground black pepper to taste, then mix.

Add the hot pasta to the mozzarella salad and mix well. Add the rocket/arugula, turn once. Sprinkle with olive oil and balsamic vinegar and serve warm.

Variation

Add toasted pine nuts or finely chopped garlic to the mozzarella and tomatoes. Finely chop 2 handfuls flat-leaf parsley, mint and basil, and use instead of the rocket/arugula. Omit the balsamic vinegar.

ricotta, cinnamon and walnut sauce

250 g/1 generous cup fresh ricotta

75 g/5 tablespoons unsalted butter, softened

1 teaspoon icing/confectioners' sugar

1 teaspoon ground cinnamon or mixed/apple pie spice

5 tablespoons chopped walnuts

sea salt and freshly ground black pepper

To serve

freshly cooked pasta of your choice (see page 140), reserving about 6 tablespoons of the cooking water

1½ tablespoons chopped walnuts

freshly grated Parmesan

Serves 4–6

A delicate and original dinner party dish and an ideal vegetarian option, this recipe is so simple, it can be prepared in the time it takes to cook the pasta. The combination of sweet and savoury elements dates back to Roman times and remained popular until the seventeenth century. Honey, butter, cheese and sweet spices were put together in all sorts of dishes and may well have constituted the first pasta dressing, each ingredient being added separately.

Put the ricotta, butter, icing/confectioners' sugar and cinnamon in a bowl and beat with a wooden spoon until smooth and creamy. Add salt and pepper to taste and stir 3 tablespoons of the reserved pasta cooking water.

Add the ricotta mixture to the freshly cooked pasta, add the remaining 3 tablespoons pasta water if necessary, then stir in the chopped walnuts. Mix well until coated. Serve immediately with extra walnuts and Parmesan.

Variation

Try toasted pine nuts or almonds instead of walnuts.

parma ham, rocket and bubbling blue cheese

The Parma ham crisps up beautifully in a non-stick frying pan/skillet. Other cured hams can also be used, such as serrano, San Daniele or speck.

2 tablespoons olive oil

8 slices Parma ham

200 g/1½ cups cherry tomatoes

2 Bresse Blue or mini Cambazola cheeses, 150 g/5 oz each

2 tablespoons Marsala wine or sweet sherry

2 tablespoons chopped fresh flat-leaf parsley

a handful of rocket/arugula

sea salt and freshly ground black pepper

freshly cooked pasta of your choice (see page 140) to serve

Serves 4

Heat a little of the oil in a non-stick frying pan/skillet, add the Parma ham and cook for 1 minute on each side until crisp. Remove and drain on paper towels. Add the remaining oil to the pan. When hot, add the cherry tomatoes and cook for 3–4 minutes until split and softened.

Meanwhile, cut each cheese in half crossways, put cut side up under an overhead grill/broiler and cook for 2–3 minutes, until golden and bubbling.

Break the Parma ham into pieces and add to the tomato pan. Add the Marsala and parsley and salt and pepper to taste.

Cook and drain the pasta well and return it to the warm pan. Add the Parma ham and tomato mixture and toss gently to mix. Divide between 4 bowls or plates and sprinkle with rocket. Using a spatula, slide a bubbling cheese half on top of each. Sprinkle with black pepper and serve immediately.

herby ricotta, pine nut and parmesan sauce

6 tablespoons olive oil

100 g/1 cup pine nuts

2 large handfuls rocket/arugula, chopped

2 tablespoons chopped fresh flat-leaf parsley

2 tablespoons chopped fresh basil

250 g/1 generous cup fresh ricotta

50 g/¼ cup freshly grated Parmesan cheese

sea salt and cracked black pepper

freshly cooked pasta of your choice (see page 140), to serve, reserving 4 tablespoons of the pasta cooking water

Serves 4

Pasta is the archetypal fast food. This one is fast and fresh, with the ricotta melting into the hot pasta and coating it in a creamy sauce. The pine nuts give it crunch, while the herbs lend a fresh, scented flavour. If you don't have all the herbs listed here, use just rocket plus one other – the parsley or basil suggested, or perhaps chives, snipped with scissors.

Heat the olive oil in a frying pan/skillet, add the pine nuts and fry gently until just golden. Remove from the heat but leave in the pan and set aside until needed.

Drain the cooked pasta and return both to the pan with the reserved pasta cooking water. Add the pine nuts (and their olive oil), the herbs, ricotta, half the Parmesan and plenty of cracked black pepper. Stir until evenly coated.

Serve immediately with the remaining Parmesan sprinkled on top.

choosing dried pasta

There's a huge selection of dried pasta shapes, sizes and lengths available. These can be divided into basic categories of strands, ribbons, tubes and shapes. Your choice will largely depend on the type of sauce you are serving with it. Strands (such as spaghetti) and ribbons (such as fettuccine) are ideal paired with fine and oil-based sauces, which coat the strands evenly. Tubes (such as penne) or shapes (such as conchiglie) go well with chunky or meaty sauces, as they nestle together in the bowl and catch the sauce inside their shapes. But these are just guidelines, not a set of rules – there will always be exceptions, so you should choose pairings that you like or that simply suit your mood.

Strands and ribbons

Long pasta, known as 'pasta lunga', comes either as long strands (hollow or solid) or as flat ribbons, called 'fettucce'.
Strands: spaghetti, spaghettini and bucatini – which are hollow.
Ribbons: tagliatelle, linguine, tagliolini, fettuccine and pappardelle.

Tubes and Shapes

Tubes and shapes are either plain or ridged – 'rigati'. The ridges help the sauce cling to the pasta.
Tubes: penne, chifferi, rigatoni, macaroni and maccheroni.
Shapes: fusilli, conchiglie, farfalle, orecchiette and gemelli.

Pasta for soups

Very small shapes are ideal for soups, as they look very pretty and delicate and don't dominate the soup.
Soup pasta: anellini, fedelini, stelline, alfabetini and ditali.

Pasta for baking

Lasagne are flat sheets of pasta, layered with sauce in baked dishes.
Cannelloni are large tubes for stuffing and baking.

Flavoured pasta

Dried pasta flavoured and coloured with spinach, tomato or squid ink are the most common, although beetroot/beet, herb and saffron flavours are also available.

Buying pasta

Stock up when you visit your favourite Italian deli. You can be sure any shop serving an Italian community will have a good range of top-quality, Italian-made pasta at a reasonable price and lots of shapes to choose from. Designer pasta in funky shapes and colours makes a fun gift, but stick to basics when shopping for yourself.

No need, either, to buy fresh pasta (other than the stuffed variety). Good-quality, Italian-made, dried egg pasta is better than most bought fresh pasta and it is what Italians use most of the time. Always check the labelling to make sure it's made in Italy – some manufacturers in other countries do not have the same exacting standards. If you make your own pasta, it's fantastic (see pages 133–137), but be prepared – it's two hours in the making, two minutes in the eating!

1 Canneloni

2 Penne

3 Conchiglie

4 Spaghetti

5 Anellini

6 Fusilli

7 Tagliatelle

making fresh pasta

200 g/1⅔ cups plain/all-purpose white flour (or use Italian '00' flour)

a pinch of fine sea salt

1 tablespoon olive oil

2 eggs (UK medium, US large)

Serves 2–4, depending on size of portion

Although dried pasta is perfectly good you may occasionaly want to impress with homemade so here is a basic recipe. These quantities are only guidelines – depending on humidity, type of flour used etc, you may have to add more or less flour. The dough must not be too soft – it should require some serious effort when kneading! However, too much flour will make the pasta tough to handle and when cooked, taste floury. Generally allow 1 egg to 100 g/¾ cup flour quantity per portion. However, it is not really worth the effort making a single quantity – make a large batch and once cut and shaped you can simply freeze what you do not use for another time. This basic dough can be flavoured (see page 139).

To make the pasta the traditional way, sift the flour directly onto a clean work surface (some home cooks keep a special wooden pasta board for this) and make a well in the centre with your fist.

1 Break the eggs into the well and add a pinch of salt and freshly ground black pepper and the oil.

2 Gradually mix the eggs into the flour with the fingers of one hand, and bring it together into a firm dough. If the dough looks too dry, add a few drops of water, if too wet – more flour. You will soon get to know your dough!

3 Knead the pasta until smooth, lightly massage it with a hint of olive oil, put into a plastic food bag and allow to rest for at least 30 minutes before attempting to roll out. The pasta will be much more elastic after it has had resting time.

4 Roll out in a pasta machine (see page 134) or by hand (see pages 135–137) and use as required or freeze on the day it is made.

using a pasta machine

Once you've mastered using a pasta machine, it will give you great results and take the hard work out of rolling out pasta dough.

Feed the rested dough 4–5 times through the widest setting of a pasta machine, folding in three each time, and feeding the open ends through the rollers to push out any air. This will finish the kneading process and make the pasta silky smooth.

Next, pass the pasta through the machine, starting at the widest setting first, then reducing the settings, one by one, until reaching the required thickness. The pasta sheet will become very long – so if you are having trouble, cut in it two and feed each half separately. Generally the second from last setting is best for tagliatelle, the finest being for ravioli or pasta that is to be filled – but this depends on your machine.

Once the required thickness is reached, hang the pasta over a broom handle or the back of a chair to dry a little – this will make cutting it easier in humid weather, as it will not be so sticky. Alternatively, dust with a little flour and lay out flat on clean linen cloths. Note that ravioli should be made straight away as it needs to be soft and slightly sticky to cut and fill.

To finish, pass the pasta through the chosen cutters then drape the cut pasta over the broom handle again to dry a little and lose any stickiness, until ready to cook. Alternatively, toss the cut pasta lightly in semolina flour and lay out in loose bundles on a tray lined with a clean linen cloth. Use as soon as possible before it sticks together.

making pasta shapes by hand

Simple pasta shapes can easily be made by hand. From squares or crescents for stuffed pastas, to ribbons in various thicknesses.

Macaroni

In Italy macaroni is the generic term for any hollow pasta shape. This simple-to-make version is called 'garganelle'. Use a long wooden rolling pin to roll the rested pasta dough out thinly to a rectangle on a lightly floured surface or roll out using a pasta machine. Cut squares from the pasta sheets and wrap around a pencil or chopstick on the diagonal to form tubes. Slip off and allow to dry slightly on a tray or semolina floured linen cloth before cooking.

Pappardelle

Use a long wooden rolling pin to roll the rested pasta dough out thinly on a lightly floured surface or roll out using a pasta machine (see opposite). Using a fluted pastry wheel, cut into wide ribbons. Hang up to dry a little before cooking.

Tortellini

Use a long wooden rolling pin to roll out the rested pasta dough out thinly on a lightly floured surface or roll out using a pasta machine (see opposite). Using a round cookie cutter, stamp out rounds of pasta. Pipe or spoon your chosen filling into the middle of each round. Brush the edges with beaten egg and carefully fold the round into a crescent shape, excluding all air. Bend the two corners round to meet each other and press well to seal. Repeat with the remaining dough. Leave to dry on a semolina floured linen cloth for about 30 minutes before cooking.

Ravioli

Cut the rested dough in half and wrap one half in clingfilm/plastic wrap. Use a long wooden rolling pin to roll the pasta out thinly on a lightly floured surface or roll out using a pasta machine (see opposite). Cover with a clean linen cloth or clingfilm/plastic wrap and repeat with the remaining dough. Pipe or spoon small mounds (each about 5 ml/1 teaspoon) of filling in even rows, spacing them at 4-cm/1½-inch intervals across one piece of the dough. Using a pastry brush, brush the spaces of dough between the mounds with beaten egg. Using a rolling pin, lift the remaining sheet of pasta over the mounds. Press down firmly between the pockets of filling, pushing out any trapped air. Cut into squares with a serrated ravioli/pastry cutter or a sharp knife. Transfer to a floured linen cloth to rest for about 1 hour before cooking.

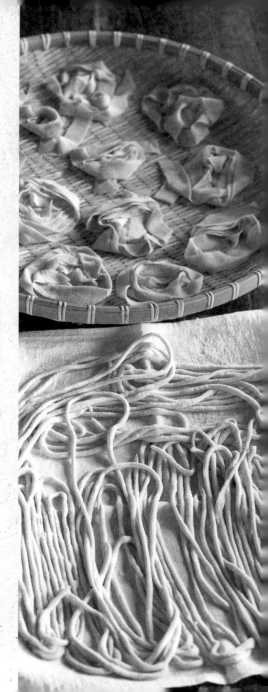

Tagliatelle

These long flat pasta noodles have endless width variations (such as linguine, tagliolini, fettuccine and pappardelle) and are probably the simplest shape to make by hand. Start by rolling the rested pasta dough out into sheets. Do this on a lightly floured surface with a long wooden rolling pin or with a pasta machine (see page 134).

1 Roll or fold one end loosely towards the centre of the sheet, then do the same with the other so that they almost meet in the middle. Lift one folded side on top of the other – do not press down on the fold.

2 Working quickly and deftly with one motion, cut into thin slices with a sharp knife, down the length of the folded pasta. A narrow noodle is tagliatelle and a wider noodle is generally considered to be pappardelle.

3 Immediately unravel the slices (or they will stick together) to reveal the pasta ribbons – you can do this by inserting the back of a large knife and shaking them loose. Hang to dry a little before cooking or

4 Dust well with semolina flour and arrange in loose 'nests' on a flat basket or a tea tray lined with a clean linen towel.

Note: These tagliatelle noodles can be used straightaway or bagged up, sealed and stored in the freezer for up to up to 1 month. It can be cooked from frozen – simply drop straight into a large pan of salted boiling water until al dente then drain and serve immediately with the sauce of your choice.

flavouring pasta

Fresh pasta dough can be flavoured with a variety of simple ingredients. They add a subtle flavour and often, an enticing and appetizing colour.

Green herb pasta

Add at least 3 tablespoons finely chopped fresh soft green herbs (such as basil, flat-leaf parsley or coriander/cilantro) to the well in the flour. Or blanch the herbs, dry, then chop before use.

Tomato pasta

Add 2 tablespoons tomato purée/paste or sun-dried tomato paste to the well in the flour. Use 1 UK large/US extra large egg instead of 2 UK medium/US large ones.

Saffron pasta

Soak a sachet of powdered saffron in 2 tablespoons hot water for 15 minutes. Use 1 UK large/US extra large egg instead of 2 UK medium/US large ones and whisk in the saffron-infused water.

Black squid ink pasta

Add 1 sachet of squid ink to the eggs before adding to the flour. A little extra flour may be needed.

Beetroot pasta

Add 2 tablespoons grated cooked beetroot/beet to the well in the flour. Use 1 UK large/US extra large egg instead of 2 UK medium/US large.

cooking pasta

Cooking times for both dried and fresh pasta vary according to the size, type and quality of the pasta. The only way to be sure is to taste it (and be guided by the manufacturer's instructions). However, the basic methods of cooking remains the same so here are some guidelines.

How much pasta to cook?

How much pasta you cook depends on whether the pasta is a first or main course/entrée and how hungry you and your family or guests are. As a guide, you should allow the following quantity per person:

75–115 g/3–4 oz dried pasta
115–150 g/4–5 oz fresh pasta
175–200 g/6–7 oz fresh filled pasta
(such as ravioli or tortelloni)

Cooking dried pasta

• Cook pasta in a large saucepan or pot with plenty of salted, boiling water. Don't skimp on the salt, or the pasta will taste bland – add it to the water just before you add the pasta.

• Add the pasta to the boiling water all at once.

• Keep the water boiling and cook with the lid off. Stir with a wooden fork to stop it sticking, but don't add olive oil to the water: it's a waste of oil!

• Don't overdrain and never rinse cooked pasta – the coat of starch helps the sauce cling. Reserve a cupful or so of pasta cooking water (or the quantity dictated by the recipe you are following) before you drain, then add it to the sauce pasta to keep it warm or to the sauce to thin it to a desired consistency if it seems a little thick.

• For an Italian the only way to serve pasta is 'al dente', which literally means 'to the tooth'. Al dente pasta is springy, almost a little elastic and should have a little resistance in the centre of the pasta when you bite down – when it is overcooked it is flabby and when undercooked has a chalky centre.

• Don't delay – pasta gets cold quickly. Return drained pasta to the warm saucepan or to a warmed serving bowl, add the sauce, toss with a fork and spoon, then serve and garnish immediately.

Cooking fresh pasta

Cook fresh pasta using the same basic method as for dried but be aware that as it is still full of moisture it needs far less cooking time; sometimes just 30 seconds is enough (though 3 minutes is about average) but read the packet instructions to be sure. If you overcook filled pasta it will burst and lose it's filling so it's best to be cautious and not leave it unattended as it cooks!

index

picture credits

Susan Bell
Page 75 insert

Martin Brigdale
Pages 7, 81, 107, 126 insert, 138, 140 left

Peter Cassidy
Pages 11 all inserts, 31, 37 insert, 38, 43 insert, 46, 54, 55 insert, 58, 59, 65, 73, 79, 112, 117 background, 128, 132–133, 134 insert, 135 right, 137, 139 insert, 140 right

Vanessa Davies
Pages 60, 66

Nicki Dowey
Pages 3, 14, 16, 19, 23, 24, 32, 35, 36, 42, 45, 49, 50, 57, 69, 70, 74, 77, 80, 82, 86, 89, 93, 97, 101, 108, 119, 123, 124, 136

Tara Fisher
Pages 29 insert, 84 insert, 85

Jonathan Gregson
Page 116

Richard Jung
Pages 1, 8 below center, 8 below right, 15, 28, 37 background, 83, 103 background, 117 insert

Lisa Linder
Page 91

William Lingwood
Pages 17 background, 40, 51, 53, 64, 105, 114, 125, 127, 131, 134 background

David Munns
Pages 8 below left, 87 insert, 141

Steve Painter
Pages 4, 8 above both, 72, 103 insert, 110, 113 insert, 121 insert, 129

William Reavell
Pages 2, 5, 21 insert, 26, 30, 34, 41, 44, 52, 71, 75 background, 78, 90, 94, 96, 98, 99, 100 insert, 104 insert, 109, 120, 122, 144

Debi Treloar
Page 17 insert, 113 background

Ian Wallace
Pages 6, 15, 20, 27, 39, 61, 62, 63, 102, 106, 111, 115

Kate Whitaker
Pages 13, 21 background, 25, 47, 76, 95, 139 background, 142–143

Clare Winfield
Pages 22, 33

recipe credits

Lindy Wildsmith
Baby clam sauce
Basic cream sauce with butter and Parmesan
Basic tomato sauce
Calabrese and broccoli arabesque
Carbonara sauce
Cherry tomatoes and mozzarella with rocket
Country sausage, pea and tomato
Grilled prawns and salmon with basil and citrus cream sauce
Herbed chicken with garlic breadcrumbs
Ligurian meat sauce with tomato, mushrooms and pine nuts
Monkfish and Italian vegetables with olives and capers
Mushroom and marsala sauce
Pork mini meatballs
Primavera
Prosciutto, Emmental and lettuce sauce
Puttanesca sauce
Quick Neapolitan tomato sauce
Ragù meat sauce
Ricotta, cinnamon and walnut sauce
Roasted vegetables with capers and cherry tomatoes
Simple garlic and chilli sauce
Spicy bacon and tomato sauce
Tuna, coriander seed and lemon zest

Louise Pickford
Bolognese sauce
Chilli tuna tartare
Foaming sage butter
Gorgonzola, pecan and mascarpone sauce
Herby ricotta, pine nut and Parmesan sauce
Lemon, cream and vermouth sauce
Rich seafood sauce
Sausagemeat ragù
Spicy roasted tomato sauce

Caroline Marson
Artichoke and almond pesto
Broccoli, anchovy, Parmesan and crème fraîche
Broccoli, Parmesan and basil pesto
Classic basil pesto
Coriander, chilli and peanut pesto
Mint, ginger and almond pesto
Red pepper and walnut pesto

Tonia George
Baby clams with tarragon and cherry tomatoes
Beef polpetti in tomato sauce
Breaded garlicky chicken with parsley
Goat cheese and basil pesto with peas
Lemon, basil and Parmesan cream sauce
Pork and lemon ragù sauce

Maxine Clark
Flavouring pasta
Making fresh pasta
Making pasta shapes by hand
Using a pasta machine

Rachel Anne Hill
Chilli scallops
Creamy artichoke, asparagus and ham sauce
Creamy bacon and mushroom carbonara

Brian Glover
Courgette, mint, lemon and cream sauce
Pan-fried squash, walnut and parsley sauce

Silvana Franco
Aubergine and tomato
Parma ham rocket and bubbling blue cheese

Clare Ferguson
Lobster sauce
Radicchio, saffron and cracked black pepper sauce

Fiona Beckett
Aubergine, sausage and zinfandel sauce

Linda Collister
Smoked salmon, crème fraîche and dill

Amanda Grant
Broad beans and bacon